CREATIVE MONEYMAKING

The Psychic Path to Abundance

A NEW EDITION

Revised and Updated by Osborne Phillips

of

THE LLEWELLYN PRACTICAL GUIDE
TO
CREATIVE MONEYMAKING

Melita Denning & Osborne Phillips

CREATIVE MONEYMAKING

The Psychic Path to Abundance

Copyright © 2015 by Osborne Phillips

All rights reserved

*No part of this book may be used or reproduced
in any manner whatsover
including Internet usage
without written permission from Osborne Phillips
except in the case of brief quotations
falling within the legal definition of 'fair dealing'*

ISBN: 1503272230
ISBN-13: 978-1503272231

A SELECTION OF OTHER BOOKS FROM DENNING AND PHILLIPS

The Magical Philosophy Series:

Book I *Robe and Ring* 1974
Book II *The Apparel of High Magic* 1975
Book III *The Sword and the Serpent* 1975
Book IV *The Triumph of Light* 1978
Book V *Mysteria Magica* 1982

(with various later Llewellyn editions of this work)

The Llewellyn Practical Guides Series:

Astral Projection 1979
CreativeVisualization 1980
Psychic Self-Defense & Well-Being 1980
The Development of Psychic Powers 1981
The Magick of the Tarot 1983
Creative Moneymaking 1992

Magic and the Holy Qabalah:

Magical States of Consciousness 1985
Planetary Magic 1989
Entrance to the Magical Qabalah 1997
*Aurum Solis:
Initiation Ceremonies & Inner Magical Techniques* 2001

Out-of-Body Experience

Astral Projection: Plain & Simple 2003

CONTENTS

1	ABUNDANCE FOR ALL	5
2	TRANQUILITY	15
3	POSITIVE SAVING	17
4	MULTI-LEVEL INTERACTION	27
5	SUBLIMINAL DYNAMICS	39
6	MONITORING THE DEEPS	49
7	YOUR TALENTS	53
8	INFUSING THE IMAGE (1)	65
9	INFUSING THE IMAGE (2)	74
10	THE CREATIVE INVESTOR	83
11	CATALOGUE OF DREAM SYMBOLS	101

PSYCHIC PRACTICES INCLUDED IN THIS BOOK

Dwelling in the Creative Light - 11

Establishing Tranquility - 15

Activating your Gain - 18

Basic Mirror Practice - 44

Increasing Psychic Energy - 55

The Fivefold Prana Sequence - 60

Infusing the Image 1 - 66

Infusing the Image 2 – 79

Blessing your Investments - 85

The Bespeaking Procedure - 88

Questioning the Deep Mind - 93

1

ABUNDANCE FOR ALL

This book is about the HEALTHY, POSITIVE, ETHICAL and LASTING creation of PERSONAL PROSPERITY.

1 - It will tell you how to build and achieve financial success without worry (because worry never created anything in the positive way of living).

2 - It will tell you how to prosper financially while improving your life and getting more interest (in both senses of the word) and real happiness out of living.

3 - It will help you enhance your psychic faculties and your inner evolution.

4 - It is also likely to motivate you to explore and develop some artistic, technical or social talents you may have neglected.

EFFECTIVE LIVING

Let's be frank about this. Money is the lifeblood of the community. The possession of money gives us our ability to live effectively: it virtually constitutes our *right* to live! In the current economic climate it is apparent that if we want to increase our prosperity we are not seeking simply to advance on a level plain: we need to make our way upwards on a 'down escalator'.

We can take this image further. Just as if we needed physically to run up a down escalator, so on this metaphorical escalator, if we are to ascend without a damaging strain on nerves and heart, it's highly desirable to have wings!

Material resources are not enough. With regard to our financial status, the Healthy, Positive, Ethical and Lasting Creation of Prosperity provides the wings.

IS THIS FOR YOU?

You may be just starting out on a career, or you may be heading towards retirement. You may have the prospect of a pension which looked good a few years back but which seems painfully little now. Or you may have done well, saved and invested, but the interest rates are barely holding against inflation and taxation and you don't want to sit helplessly watching the erosion. Or you may be prospering, but may still feel it isn't the best you can do.

Or you may simply have acquired this book for something to read, without seriously thinking that Creating Prosperity might be for you. Well, in any of these cases and in plenty of others, Creating Prosperity definitely is for you.

All you need is to decide that really, truly and deeply, you want to Create Prosperity.

THE COSMIC FLOW

This decision means, effectively, that you want to participate in the balance and the harmonious and unimpeded interaction of the life-forces, thereby opening the gates to the blessings of universal abundance.

THE WISH AND THE WILL

Probably in a general way most people *wish* they had more money than they have. But to *will*, specifically, to make money – to see yourself as a creator of prosperity, albeit perhaps a newly-fledged one – that is another matter.

It call for an attitude of mind which is both RESOLVED and ATTENTIVE. It may come to you all complete in a flash and thereafter be yours for life, or, likely enough, you may have to practice it until it becomes a settled habit of thought and feeling. There is much in this book to help you establish that habit, but the chief thing is *the way you see yourself*. You are a **producer of necessary resources**, and soon you will be a **CREATOR OF PROSPERITY**. Keep this in mind.

This doesn't mean that Prosperity is created by heroic will power. No creative endeavour is. The will, of itself, has no controlling power over the creative levels within the psyche. Certainly you will use your will in many of the steps towards your goal: to bring back your attention if it wanders, to direct your visualization to what you intend, or to complete a process of relaxation, for example. But for perseverance and success in your main enterprise, Creating Prosperity, you will evoke for yourself the powerful persuasions of

VISION and IMAGINATION, so that you may hardly be conscious of the work of the will.

Consider Columbus' first Atlantic voyage. People sometimes think and write of it as if the courageous navigator hauled himself and his sailors across thousands of miles of untried ocean, with all the perils, hardships and sufferings of the endeavour, simply by stark will power.

That way, he would not even have been able to get his crew aboard. Columbus was a man of immense vision and imagination, with the power to impart his perceptions to others. It was that vision and imagination which won over the Castilian queen to sell her jewels: it was that vision and imagination which gathered his crew, and which maintained the arduous enterprise to its conclusion.

It was that same vision and imagination within his soul which kept his own will unswerving.

GUARD YOUR INSTRUMENTS

Your own vision and imagination, as you will see more and more clearly as you progress, are your vital and essential 'instruments' in the Creation of Prosperity, and you can allow nobody to tamper with them. The phony 'reasons' to lure you to purchase this or that unnecessary article, or to fall into this or that tourist trap, are presented vividly to your imagination. Your task is to blot out the presented ideas by turning your attention and your emotions at once to your true goal and purpose: not as an act of self-denial but as a traveller's swift glance at the inward picture of a loved destination.

Again, in this book you will find help to achieve this swift turning of the imagination, which is your chief defense against all who would tempt you to squander your precious resources of money, time or talent.

A DANGEROUS MISTAKE

If you don't already have the outlook of a creator of prosperity, you may need to reconsider some of your attitudes of mind. If you have not yet learned to think of money as something to cultivate, you may still automatically think of it as something only to spend.

Does the news of an unexpected bonus overturn your perfectly good budget? Does it at once mean 'let's eat out tonight'? Does it mean 'Now I can give my partner a great surprise present'?

Beware! If you seek favour by spending, or if for any other reason you take *spending* as the accepted reaction to *money*, this is a dangerous mistake. This spontaneous response, 'money is for spending', has ruined not only countless individuals but also dynasties, businesses, big organizations, governments, and even empires. SPENDOMANIA has destroyed many fortunes. If you see bad examples around you, don't be misled into following them. Injudicious spending is neither clever nor amusing. Win respect for your sound sense with financial resources. This will strengthen your own positive view of yourself, and this, as a further benefit, will help you to attract and channel the inexhaustible cosmic forces of abundance into your life.

THE LODESTONE

'Gold attracts gold' is a well known observation, and it can be made to do so even more powerfully when you work on the matter. *But you yourself can become this 'Gold that attracts gold'. You can become a veritable* **Lodestone of Power** *to attract the energies of increase and prosperity.*

LIKE ATTRACTS LIKE

You know that if you want to attract pieces of ferrous metal (iron or steel) with a physical magnet, it has to be made of ferrous metal. Then the pieces of metal will become magnetized and attract more in their turn. Aluminium or silver cannot be made to attract iron or steel. Again: solutions of certain chemicals (sodium thiosulphate, for example) will crystallize into solidity at once if a small crystal of their own kind is placed in them. No substance but their own will do it, but a tiny fragment of their own kind, which has their own molecular and crystalline structure, is enough to set in operation in the liquid the mysterious lines of attraction which cause it to solidify forthwith.

As with inanimate things, so also with living beings. A happy face sets others smiling. 'If you want to have a friend', says the proverb, 'you must be a friend'. The people of the Stone Ages probably lived in much closer unity with the natural world than any of their descendants. Their cave paintings usually began at a place on wall or roof where some irregularity in the rock suggested a shape – perhaps an animal head – to the imagination of the artist. Once he had improved on that likeness (the students of cave art point out) his creativity and that of others was stimulated to spread wonderfully animated shapes across the surface.

The principles runs through the whole world of life, at every level. It is well known that to induce hens to lay their eggs in a particular place, you need to put a dummy egg in the intended nest. This, incidentally, is the exact reason why a sum of money put aside is called a 'nest-egg'. It is not merely hoarded as a treasure. The intention is that other sums should be attracted to join it in the 'nest'.

So you need to become an effective Lodestone, a focus and a channel for the cosmic powers of abundance. You need, in fact, to become a person in dynamic harmony with the powers of abundance at all levels of your being.

Think about the principle LIKE ATTRACTS LIKE. Richer earth produces better crops. A good leader builds a good team. Happy folk radiate happiness, and good news is a tonic. St. Paul's letter to the Philippians (4: 8) tells the community, *Whatsoever things are of good report ...... think on these things.*

So your first step in this harmonization is to set the appropriate forces in motion at a high level, filling your psyche with the spiritual powers of abundance and fullness of life. Here is a sound technique for this purpose:

DWELLING IN THE CREATIVE LIGHT

Preparation

1 - Stand in a place where you can be quiet and alone.

2 – Close your eyes. Calm your mind, allowing all discursive thought, all concerns, to fade from your awareness.

3 - Know that you are a being at peace. Know that you are a child of earth and heaven, and that you are the center and focus of all the worlds of light and life.

Practice

1 – Visualize yourself surrounded, enveloped, by an ovoid,

an aura, of bright blue light. (*You don't have to be able to see this as if with your physical eyes, but you should be definite as to its shape, colour and brightness.*)

2 – Now, within this blue aura, visualize, just above your head but not touching it, a small sphere of shining white light. This light is a symbol of your highest and inmost self.

3 – Remaining aware of the blue aura and the shining white light at its summit, turn your thoughts to the highest and noblest principles of which you can conceive: whether Goodness, Beauty and Truth; Celestial Light; Divine love; the Divine Mind; or simply God; or some other positive, inspiring and transcendent concept that stirs you personally.

4 – As you raise your mental gaze to contemplation of these things, visualize the sphere of shining white light at the summit of your aura becoming brighter and ever brighter until its radiance floods forth to fill your aura with white brilliance. When you are ready, say, aloud or mentally.

I DWELL IN THE LIGHT

LIGHT SURROUNDS ME

LIGHT FILLS ME AND MOVES WITHIN ME

I AM ONE WITH THE LIGHT

5 – Remaining aware of the light-filled aura, now imagine yourself growing larger in stature, becoming vast, vast, immeasurably vast.

6 – In this ambience, turn your mind specifically to the beneficent powers of abundance and increase, great and inexhaustible cosmic forces that flood ever into the universe

and into your psyche, and to which you can respond with warmth and welcome. *By affirming your awareness of these powers, you are enhancing their activity and potency within your psyche.* When you are ready, in your mighty, light-filled aura proclaim, aloud or mentally:

I AM A LODESTONE FOR ABUNDANCE

I AM A CHANNEL FOR ABUNDANCE

I AM ONE WITH THE FORCES OF ABUNDANCE

7 – Maintaining the sense of vastness and light, enjoy for as long as you wish the inner awareness of peace, of power, of your potential for psychic achievement.

8 - When you are ready, allow these formulations to fade from your consciousness, and then open your eyes.

BENEFITS OF THE TECHNIQUE

Perform this simple practice of 'Dwelling in the Creative Light' every day, at whatever time suits you. It will not take long to do, particularly when you can do it from memory.

Even before you begin to establish your programme for creating prosperity on a more material basis, you are likely to benefit considerably from the technique of 'Dwelling in the Creative Light'. For you will be bringing yourself into an ever greater harmony with the creative cosmic power of abundance, the power of fullness of life at all levels. Later, when you have the various aspects of your programme running harmoniously together, the benefits will be enhanced. But, even at the beginning, when the powers of increase have nothing in which to 'earth' themselves, except your own physical and emotional makeup, you can begin to notice within yourself – and very likely in external happenings also – some effects of your new attitude to living. A subtle but definite increase in your vitality should become apparent, and your imaginative faculties should be enhanced.

Even if you are already prosperous, it's a good thing to stop any useless little acts of extravagance and waste. Now you will find it easier to stop. Why? Because most people who feel impelled to keep certain useless extravagances in their life do so *in order to boost their self-confidence*. (You may have noticed with some people, the more worried they become about money matters the more acts of senseless extravagance they commit.)

With the help of the technique of 'Dwelling in the Creative Light' – which is the essential foundation on which the further techniques given in this book are established – you will be developing your *true* self-confidence and will have no need to bolster it with pretences. You will treat your resources carefully, as any responsible person does.

There is also another very positive side to the beginning you are making here. *As soon as you treat your resources with care and respect, more will begin coming to you.*

Remember, 'Gold attracts gold'. This is the first basic principle of creating prosperity. The attraction may show itself in quite small gains at first, but it really happens.

The **Lodestone** is beginning to work, under the royal and highly potent cosmic forces of **prosperity** and **increase**. So, from day to day, make a point of noticing your progress as a Creator of Prosperity: sums of money which come to you, increases in your savings, toughening of your resistance against useless spending. Notice, and be spurred to further endeavours.

2

TRANQUILITY

In this book you will sometimes find a reminder to relax. It's needful at that point that you put any stressful thoughts and feelings out of the way so as to give entire attention to what you are going to do. *How* you relax should be your decision. If you are completely relaxed to begin with, simply go on as you are. Or if you can just close your eyes, take a deep breath and relax, that's fine too. The simple relaxation technique which follows, however, is for use whenever you feel in need of a deeper level of detachment from the stress of circumstances.

ESTABLISHING TRANQUILITY

1 - If you wish, have some specific, gentle music, or sounds of nature that you find soothing, quietly playing as a background for your relaxation.

2 – In creating a calm atmosphere you may find it helpful to burn some incense that suggests to you the sacred, or that you associate with peace, or with a restful ambience, or with some other equable quality. Your incense can be in the form of cones, or sticks, or in granular form to be burned on charcoal.

1 – Lie flat on your back on a rug, exercise mat or firm mattress. Close your eyes. Sink your chin a little towards your chest, so as to rest steadily on the back of your neck.

2 – Take a few slow, deep breaths while you settle into this posture. Throughout this relaxation procedure, go on breathing deeply and evenly as though you were asleep

3 – Beginning with your toes and working upwards, first flex and then relax the muscles of each portion of your body in turn: toes, feet, calves, thighs, hips, buttocks, abdomen, chest, shoulders, arms, hands, neck, head and face.

4 – If during the relaxation your mind strays to other matters, bring your attention gently back to the simple physical actions you are performing. The more complete your attention, the better you will relax.

5 – When you have relaxed your head and face, turn your attention back to your toes. Check over each part of your body in sequence, to make sure each is still fully relaxed.

6 – Maintain your rhythmic breathing and lie relaxed in the same posture for as long as you wish, mentally saying to yourself, one or many times:

PEACE SURROUNDS ME

PEACE IS WITHIN ME

I AM A BEING AT PEACE

3

POSITIVE SAVING

Saving is not merely the grade school for prosperity. It is the backbone of prosperity. There is not only the obvious truth that money saved is money gained. There is also the less obvious but more vital fact that the continual habit of saving sharpens the appetite for having more to save. It helps you attain the mental attitude of the Creator of Prosperity.

THE PRINCIPLE OF INCREASE

Once more we see the working of the basic principle, that increase brings increase. Put aside a regular amount. Be serious about it, but don't be unrealistic about what you can afford to save. Putting money away and then having frequently to bring it into use a week or so later is bad practice: it's bad for your morale and it creates an atmosphere of instability. Make a sensible decision as to what you can save, and then stay firmly with it. But add also to your savings, without delay, any extra amount that comes to you unless it is definitely needed for a good purpose.

When you have anything to add to your savings, particularly when it's an extra or unexpected gain, it's a good thing to signify your attunement with the cosmic Forces of Abundance and to bless, 'fertilize', the specific amount by the following method.

ACTIVATING YOUR GAIN

1 – In a convenient place set up a small table or pedestal, covered with a drape of bright blue, or of blue and gold.

2 - Place upon this table the money you are adding to your savings, or place upon it whatever document signifies the amount that has come to you.

1 – Lay your hands upon the money, statement or cheque, or whatever, and say:

I WELCOME THIS INCREASE

I ASSIGN IT TO THE FORCES OF COSMIC ABUNDANCE

SO SHALL IT PROSPER

2 - Standing before the table, now perform the spiritual practice of 'Dwelling in the Creative Light'. Do not proceed at once to step 8 of this technique, however, but remain in step 7 while you perform the following actions.

3 – Thus, maintaining the sense of vastness and light, and enjoying the inner awareness of peace and power and potential for psychic achievement, hold your hands palm downward above the new sum of money or whatever represents it, and keeping your eyes closed, say:

I TAKE THIS INCREASE TO MY STORE

SO SHALL IT GROW AND SUMMON MORE

SO SHALL IT FLOURISH MIGHTILY

BLESSED BY DIVINE PROSPERITY

4 - When you are ready, withdraw your hands. Then, as in step 8 of 'Dwelling in the Creative Light', allow the formulations to fade from your consciousness, and open your eyes.

AN INTERPERSONAL HURDLE

In becoming a Positive Saver and a Creator of Prosperity you are to a greater or lesser extent going to change. That in fact is what you intend.

You are not at all likely to change in any of your basic ideas and opinions, political, religious or other. There's no reason why you should. You may change in your attitude to some of the material things of life. You will very likely – and rightly – develop a higher and more positive opinion of yourself. In certain respects you may very likely improve your health.

If you have a life partner and the two of you are of one mind about Positive Saving and Creating Prosperity, there will be no problem about the changes involved, and in fact your partnership will be a highly potent force at all levels.

In some instances however this unity of purpose does not immediately exist. Rules cannot be laid down for handling a situation of that kind. Should you be faced with it, the best and strongest hope for a good solution lies in your own quiet perseverance, your complete and positive adherence to your own creative programme.

Don't on any account give up on that. Don't be fanatical about it either. Those qualities have no place in the Creative Way.

You have to bear in mind that many people – not only a life partner but also friends, workmates, even quite casual acquaintances – may intensely dislike to see anyone change from the way they've known them. To stop smoking, go on a diet, or even change one's hairstyle will often arouse a storm of protest. You see this everywhere.

Why do people act like that? *Simply because they are afraid.* People of a different kind (people who want to improve their health or like to try a new look, and Creators of Prosperity such as you) have a progressive, ongoing view of life. These people know that life really consists in going forward, changing, developing. But those who are afraid take a fixed, stationary view of life. They want everything to stay as it is, which is in any case impossible. They try all they can to keep the people around them from changing.

So when people notice you changing in some of your ways, if they try to cajole or bully you into a return, don't get angry, don't argue – BUT DON'T EVER GO BACK ON YOUR TRACKS!

POSITIVE SAVING HELPS POSITIVE LIVING

Positive Saving not only helps you save. It also encourages you to decide how much you will spend. Another important development is that you will take an increasingly clear and realistic view as to what you *truly* want to spend *on*.

Every person should be able to put aside some sum of money, however small, on a regular basis as long-term savings. If you really can't, then you ought to see if you can find a subsidiary source of income – again, however small – which can be devoted to this purpose.

The snare, you see, is the mistaken idea that such a small amount 'isn't worth saving'.

Small amounts ARE worth saving because –

1 - They add up into large amounts.

2 - They boost your morale. You are a *saver*.

3 - They give you special opportunities to invoke the Powers of Increase by *Activating Your Gain*.

Additionally to these points, some people have a bad habit of labeling as 'small amounts', and squandering, what are really quite sizeable amounts. To guard against that, 'looking after the pennies' is good practice.

HOW MUCH?

Individual and family circumstances make big variations in what is *possible* to save and what is *desirable* to save, and no model budget can be worked out to suit everyone.

If you live alone and you aspire to being a 'hard-saver', there's no reason against it. Indeed a person alone can receive such severe knocks in life that hard saving can be of special value to them. Wherever and whoever you, you have no right to endanger your health by allowing yourself insufficient food, clothing or heating, neither would such extremism be in harmony with the principles of creativity. Nevertheless, a person can often live healthily and happily on a budget which would startle the neighbours.

If you are one of a family group, the situation is more complex. Doubtless you derive benefits from being a member of a larger unit, while paying your share towards the family care, food budget, utilities and so on. But there may be areas where you can legitimately save, and are able to do so without giving offence. Even if you have to limit your saving to the field of your own personal living and spending, you can still do well.

If you are one of a couple, the two of you need to give the subject of saving some serious consideration. This needs real honesty with each other, which will help each of you to be honest with yourself. Nobody should take the fun out of anyone's life. Equally, you don't need to give your partner the 'pleasure' of buying you something you don't really want, when both of you in truth would rather save the money.

It may be a good time to consider some new activities, too. Routine pleasures and entertainments have taken creativity right out of many people's lives, while perhaps not pleasing or entertaining any longer. If you can spare a little outlay to develop a craft or a skill which attracts you, you may find a new means of saving money, as for instance through DIY home repairs, or through an online business you set up to market your skills.

THE PROSPEROUS SAVER'S PROBLEM

Prosperity is a most favourable quality to have and to enjoy. It has many advantages, but one noticeable disadvantage: *it can take the sharp edge off the motivation to save.*

This need not happen. To watch the steady and meaningful increase in one's capital can be, in itself, an added incentive, a spur to even greater efforts.

That is the key. To watch the increase. If, instead, one is watching catalogues that offer glamour items, fashion accessories, property, cars and suchlike, there's a temptation to say all too easily, 'Do you know, now we could afford ......'

Not *'We need ......'* or *'Our lifestyle might be improved by......'* but just *'We could afford ......'* As your capital increases, you'll be able to *afford* many things which once seemed out of reach, but which you don't necessarily need or even, truly, wish for.

THE LUMP-SUM SAVER'S PROBLEM

If a lump sum suddenly comes your way, over and above your routine savings, how will you handle it? It may be a surprise bonus which will naturally go into your normal savings account, or it may be a larger sum – a substantial legacy, for instance – which you may want to invest.

Either way, it may not reach its destination whole and intact.

In this sort of case, the danger lies not so much in the catalogues or the sales talk: *the temptation is the money itself.* You decide to carve a bit off, and then look around for something to spend it on. Chances are, the thing you decide on will cost a little more than the amount you intended, so you carve a bit more off. This is the operative factor which you can introduce at once into your programme.

Now, for a non-routine gain of this sort, it's reasonable to use some of it *to fill an existing need*; but that is quite another thing from the temptation to 'spend for the sake of spending'. The matter calls for responsible decisions. For self-employed people, and others whose savings are mainly of the lump-sum variety, it is a recurring matter for care.

THE SOLUTION TO THE PROBLEM

For almost everyone, the path of Positive Saving is beset by obstacles, some of them incidental, some deliberately placed by people who count on gaining from your weakness. In all the instances we've suggested, the solution to the problem lies, not in the outer world, but within yourself.

BEGIN WITH YOURSELF

You have seen the importance of Vision and Imagination. Now you might take a closer look at the inner processes of imagination, since the way you use your imagination is *a major controlling factor in how you spend or save.*

As your imagination can lead your emotions, so your emotions can lead your thinking and your actions.

This may be a startling fact, but you can turn it to very good advantage.

At first you may feel it does an injustice to your reasoning faculty. Certainly your thinking and your actions don't have to be led by every impulse presented by your imagination. An attractive advertisement doesn't send you dashing instantly to buy a certain pizza, or to book a flight on a certain airline. But it may lead you to consider the particular thing advertised with a degree of attention which can well sway your choice when a time for decision arrives. This in itself can be useful. A great deal of our understanding of everyday matters comes from advertisements.

It is important, however, that you should be *aware* of the sequence of motivation:

Attention – Imagination – Emotion - Thought or Action

For one thing, you can guard against its leading you to do something which was no part of your well-considered plans, or to spend money you would not otherwise have spent.

But your awareness of the sequence of motivation gives you a greater advantage even than that, a much more positive advantage.

You can use this knowledge to shape your own life and actions. As an example, there is the matter of self-image.

WHO ARE YOU?

No matter whether you see yourself primarily as a car owner, a homemaker or a dog lover, a musician, business person or sports fan, you know there are numberless objects, many of them poorly designed, childish or just plain overpriced, offered specially for 'you' to wear, drink from, keep on your desk or in your car, or install in your home as a dust collector.

Things of that sort are a temptation to many people, who buy them on impulse usually not because of any intrinsic attractiveness, but because the things help them feel they've 'joined the club' - are actively being this or that kind of person.

Well, if this example applies to you, you can guard against it by reminding yourself that whatever other interests you may have, you've also joined another 'club' now: *you are a Creator of Prosperity.*

RENEW YOUR DEFENCES

Frequently perform the spiritual practice of 'Dwelling in the Creative Light'; and when you go to visit the stores, or you are about to leaf through a catalogue, visualize just above your head the small sphere of shining white light that represents your higher self, and say to yourself:

I AM A CREATOR OF PROSPERITY

I AM A POSITIVE SAVER

Use your power of Vision and Imagination to promote your own real objective. Don't allow other folks to make you see and feel what *they* want you to.

4

MULTI-LEVEL INTERACTION

What's the difference between an enthusiastic Creator of Prosperity and a miser? You might say it is the difference between a magnificent living creature and a prehistoric fossil. Only the fossil, being a few million years old, is necessarily a fossil, whereas the miser ought rightly to be a vital, active person still enjoying and sharing the adventures of life, and employing life's powers.

MISERLY TYPES

Drama and fiction have done a pretty good job of formulating a composite picture of the miser for us. We get the general idea of a person whose all-absorbing passion is the getting and hoarding of money. Misers may have a great deal of money or they may have little – frequently little, since they may have problems with the concept of investing it – but the don't look beyond it. They turn their back on former friends or let them drift away, and they take no interest in anyone else's concerns. Frequently their clothes and their habitations show deplorable signs of neglect.

In real life the thorough miser is a somewhat rare bird, but people with miserly tendencies show up more often. Usually they can be identified as people consciously or unconsciously embittered by having lost, or never having had, the proper development of their personal life. There are men and women left loveless because of a great disappointment or bereavement, some whose intended career has been wrecked by a physical disablement and even, occasionally, young people to whom circumstances have denied vitalizing surroundings and friends their own age. Sometimes, too, one meets with rich people who have come to shun human contacts and creative pursuits because they fear 'everyone will be after their money'.

SEALED OFF

The evident difference between these miserly people and normal prudent folk is that the miserly ones have to a greater or lesser extent *sealed themselves off* from the currents of the life-force in this world, from mental and physical activities, from the general give and take which is involved in work and play, from the interactive sharing of ideas, of help, of encouragement: but also from more than that.

Even more seriously, but probably without intending it or perceiving it, they are in process of losing contact with the higher spiritual sources of life within their own being and in the universe at large. This is the 'fossilization' process referred to earlier on. Their interests have become limited to the narrow concerns of their own lower self, and the image of material gain has become obsessive.

FETISHES

The obsessive image could perhaps have been something other than money. Some people make a 'fetish' of their bodily health and strength, some of the perfection of their home, some of moral purity; all excellent qualities but none of them adequate as the supreme governing and inspirational force in a person's life. Money, however, when it becomes a complete end in itself, excluding all other concerns, is a particularly dangerous 'fetish'.

The danger lies in the fact that to our awareness, conscious and unconscious, both rational and emotional-instinctual, the idea of money really carries immense power. Not only does money have power truly in itself, it is also the symbol and representative in our lives of much that that is truly life-giving and spiritually active.

SUNLIGHT AND LIFE-BLOOD

In the days of gold coin, money easily symbolized the light of the sun. Deep in the minds of many people this image still carries a high potency because money, like sunshine, still brings benefits which transcend the material level: hope, release from anxiety, an incentive to live and to work for the future. In an absolute sense, our life on this earth depends upon the sun: in a civilized state, our life on this earth depends upon money. Similarly, also, money symbolizes the life-blood circulating in our bodies, because it is in truth the life-blood of the body politic. Here too, it has much to do with our inner confidence, our sense of self-worth and our generous aspirations.

In many ways money not only represents the spiritual forces of life and well-being in the world, it also greatly helps their action. But that is not to imply that it can take the place of the unseen spiritual forces themselves. That is where the misers go astray.

SAFEGUARDS

You, the Creator of Prosperity, cannot let the concept of simple material money seal out the hidden reality of 'the spiritual origin of Prosperity and Increase'. But, in fact, you are not likely to seal it out, because your regular practice of 'Dwelling in the Creative Light' will powerfully enhance and continually refresh your awareness of it.

Besides, you will assuredly know from unexpected increases to your store that the material world is not an isolated capsule in which we must, or should, be kept apart from the spiritual powers. *We are a part of those powers, and they are a part of us.* To open our consciousness, our heart, our existence to the circulation of the forces of life is not a way to invite depletion, it is to let the tides of life fill us and perpetually renew us.

A POTENT AID

This brings us to the second basic principle of Creating Prosperity. The *first principle*, 'Gold attracts gold', is widely known and its truth is endorsed by the experience of many people. The *second principle* has been much less generally perceived. But it has long been known and employed with great efficacy by mystics in many parts of the world. In calling this principle into action, however, they have always veiled it in their own colours, so that it has appeared as a power-source exclusive to them. It is rarely put forth in general terms, but just as with the first principle, this one also can be stated quite simply:

A spiritual force and the symbol representing it are most powerful when brought into action together

Christianity has always made extensive and potent use of this principle. Invocation of the Divine Spirit, the life-giving Dove, for instance, is in many instances attended in the churches of the East and the West, by the use of light and flame: light and flame being symbols of the Divine Spirit.

The mere use of light and flame would not of itself invoke that power, and the Divine Spirit could certainly be invoked to act without the symbolism, but the symbolism and the invocation, when put into action together, form an ancient and mighty combination.

Again, at an initiation in the Mithraic Mysteries, a bull was sacrificed and the blood shed over the candidate. Sacrificial death is a symbol of initiation, since the candidate must give up the old life so as to take on the new. The slaying of a bull would not of itself effect initiation (and most great initiations have been, and are, performed without any blood sacrifice), but in context of the Mithraic system, in which the mythic slaying of the bull by Mithras was the central regenerative mystery, the combination of sacrifice and initiation rite conveyed a potent message of renewal to the subliminal faculties of the candidate.

The interaction of *force* and *symbol* can therefore be clearly seen:

> THE SYMBOL CHANNELS THE FORCE
> THE FORCE VITALIZES THE SYMBOL

This second principle is of boundless importance in the Creation of Prosperity.

You have seen how you yourself and your savings – your 'nest egg' – act and react in relation to the forces of Prosperity and Increase. As a Creator of Prosperity you are a LODESTONE, *a natural magnet.* Your resources are a *magnet.* As a Creator of Prosperity you know also the supreme importance of keeping the psychic and spiritual channels open.

To use the technique 'Dwelling in the Creative Light' is important. Most important however is the action and effect of the second principle in keeping the way open in your own life and being, between the dynamic spiritual level and the material level of existence. Your awareness of this principle will considerably enhance its beneficent operation within you and for you.

So RECOGNISE that money is not an end in itself. See it for what it truly is: a SYMBOL and EARTHLY INSTRUMENT of the spiritual life-force.

STAY A VITAL, WARM, TRULY LIVING BEING. What you put into life – your creative energy, the thoroughness of your activities – enhances it. And so does the zest of the enjoyment you draw from it.

Keep the activity and interest of life stirring wherever you are, whatever you are doing. The mighty, creative spiritual currents also will be stirred in your direction, and will act through the channel of *all that can nurture the expansion and evolution of your inner being.*

ALWAYS BE CONFIDENT that the wise use of your resources, whether in saving or in outlay, will channel the high forces of Abundance. These forces in turn vitalize your resources and your life.

A SOCIAL CAUTION

The social life of the Creator of Prosperity is likely, in the main, to be quiet but satisfying. To keep one's heart open does not mean opening one's doors to all comers. Neither does it mean making oneself available for long telephone conversations with the unoccupied.

Such matters need careful watching. Worse than the immediate waste of time is the encroachment – maybe unnoticed at first – upon your attention, your energies and your life.

Your time is always precious, and these seemingly harmless people will at last, more than likely, take quite merciless advantage of what they assume to be your careless good nature.

Wisely, you will be less than tolerant to people who want to pass on tittle-tattle, or who have a meandering hard-luck story, or who just want to kill time. You have your life to live. It's time they learned to live theirs, but it is not your job to teach them.

If you were to make your time (or, worse still, any of your cash) available to them, you would be doing them no true service. You would be letting yourself down badly. You would also run the risk of having to make a refusal of time or of some sort of help to a real friend.

REAL FRIENDS ARE ANOTHER MATTER

Few people have a great number of genuine friends. The number therefore is not significant, but the genuineness of the relationship is: the relationship between people who share a dominant interest or outlook and who have, besides, a real liking and respect for each other.

Such friendships are frequently based on family or marital relationships, the original relationship being enriched or transcended in time as the parties get to know each other's true worth. In any case, a certain frugality and informal atmosphere are often noticeable when real friends meet together.

A special occasion – a birthday, a wedding, an anniversary, a reunion – may call forth a special expenditure; but nobody tries to outdo another except perhaps in fun, and each respects the other's chosen way of life. The Creator of Prosperity will find that the saying **Like Attracts Like** is true of people as well as of natural forces. Congenial company will not be lacking.

In general then, the subject of money is hardly likely to be of great moment among friends except as a business topic. But there are exceptional circumstances, and here the position of the Creator of Prosperity has to be considered.

BORROWING AND LENDING

A vast proportion of business life has in the past been conducted on credit. But now the scene has changed somewhat and credit, large or small scale, is not quite the easy answer to problems that it used to be.

Even taking into account the interest rates involved, and the fact that the banks are looking microscopically at every project that is put before them, some forms of credit can still work well for you. Check only that your net gains will be worth the outlay. Mere borrowing which is outside the immediate area of viable commerce, however, is as it always has been, a thing to avoid if possible.

A sense of proportion is needed in this. In an emergency, to borrow a realistic sum of money from a colleague – for a cab fare, for example - is reasonable. But to borrow because you have exceeded your monthly budget is unreasonable.

It is unreasonable because:

1 – **It shows a lack of control over your expenses.** This would need to be put right, even if nobody else knew about it.

2 – **It is bad for your image**, your reputation as a reliable person, whether you borrow from a colleague, your landlady or anybody else. It is not only the other person who knows: YOU know, and this can undermine your valuable sense of self-worth.

3 – **The debt must be repaid promptly**, and this is going to hurt. If you readjust your budget at once, as is evidently necessary, you are still going to be 'down' by the amount of the repayment in the ensuing month. If a debt could by any means have been avoided, recovery would have been quicker.

But the objections against lending are of equal importance, and have to be a matter of keen concern to the Positive Saver and Creator of Prosperity.

The words of one of Shakespeare's characters, 'Neither a borrower or a lender be', are in one sense immediately and absolutely true. You should never become in any degree *characterised* as either 'a borrower' or 'a lender'. The first would damage both your reputation and your self-respect. The second would make you a mark for anyone seeking a 'soft touch', and it's surprising how many people can be quite unscrupulous when they find one such in their vicinity!

Apart from such things as the cab fare previously mentioned (a matter of obliging a friend or colleague with a small sum for a day or so), you are well recommended to adopt the following principles about lending:

1 – **Never lend easily.** The person can survive without the loan, or can ask someone else. Get known as a non-lender. Word may go around, and will save you a lot of hassle.

2 – **If you do lend, never lend more than you could afford to give.** This is very important. Human nature is liable to error, and circumstances can change. No matter how admirable or how dear to you a person may be, they can still find it impossible or intensely difficult to repay a debt. In such circumstances you'd hardly want to insist on payment from that person, so you yourself would be put into difficulties.

3 – If a person you feel obliged to help does genuinely and seriously need money, but the sum they need is more than you could reasonably afford to *give*, then **offer what you know you can afford and suggest they raise the balance elsewhere.** But, *whether what you offer is the whole or a part of what they need* –

DON'T OFFER IT AS A LOAN BUT AS A GIFT

There are various good points about adopting this last principle. For one thing, it will ensure that you think carefully before making the offer. For another, it will (probably) make your person think about the gravity of accepting it.

If your person is sincere and in real difficulties, he or she will accept your offer but will make a proviso, that if and when things improve they'll return the money to you anyway. You can accept the proviso, to make your friend feel comfortable. You need not doubt his or her sincerity. But remember, you *gave* the money. So don't really expect it back. If people need money, they need it!

Maybe you'll never be called upon to act this way. If you are, and if you handle the situation as suggested here, you'll be acting prudently. You'll also be acting wisely, and in harmony with the high powers of abundance you have invoked in your life. You will not be making yourself a 'lender', or your friend a 'borrower'. The matter is just a private gift between yourselves.

WELL-WISHING

As a Creator of Prosperity you can with inner strength and without sentimentality help, by the tone of your own actions, to spread the feeling of good work, good leisure, self-respect and mutual esteem in your surroundings. It all adds up to greater Prosperity and Increase. You can step this up further by a process of well-wishing.

Wish well sincerely, in both speech and thought, to those around you. In every case, either they deserve it or they need it.

TIMELESS WATCHWORDS

As Ancient Rome developed from a walled settlement to the opulent centre of a mighty empire, two words were continually exchanged among its people. They were used in greetings to friends, in salutations, and of any occasion of meeting or parting. Usually these words are translated as *Hail* and *Farewell*, but until a late era their use was not so stereotyped as the English words would imply. Take a look at the original Latin words themselves, **Ave** and **Vale**.

Ave was used not only as a greeting generally, but also in salutation to a ruler or dignitary. Literally it means PROSPER! *In a solidly material sense.* If you look back far enough, it ties up with the English verb 'to have', the French verb 'avoir', and the German verb 'haben'.

Vale means BE FIT – GOOD HEALTH! An 'invalid' is a person whose health is lacking. A 'valid' reason is a strong and cogent reason. 'Valour' is robust courage, itself a leading concept in the Roman mind.

PROSPER AND BE FIT! You can say these things, mentally at least, to all who come your way. They are potent wishes.

Being careful with money doesn't mean being hard or ungenerous in mind. Good wishes are always yours to give, so give them freely and sincerely. Many people are more psychically receptive than you might suppose. A good wish may bring a smile to someone's face, or it may prompt another to say a gentle word instead of a harsh one. So your well-wishing gets passed on. PROSPER AND BE FIT is a good old formula.

THE COSMIC BALANCE

There is one other important thing to say here before we move on, and this concerns the reciprocal counterpart to your well-wishing:

> NEVER REFUSE, NEVER RECEIVE LIGHTLY
> A BLESSING WHICH IS GIVEN TO YOU BY ANOTHER

The cosmic forces of Abundance have their own rhythms, their own patterns of cause and effect, their own laws of equilibration, and it is well to acknowledge this.

5

SUBLIMINAL DYNAMICS

In all Creation of Prosperity there is one main governing factor which you should bear in mind:

YOUR WORK
IS NOT ON THE MATERIAL LEVEL ONLY

THE INVISIBLE FACTOR

All the time you are thinking and acting as a Creator of Prosperity you are BUILDING UP A MAGNETIC TENSION in the psychic atmosphere around you. On these terms, *some major thing must in due course 'give' in your favour!* And when it gives you'll be organized and ready to receive.

The new expansion may be a promotion or it may be a new job opportunity. It may be in the area of your savings and investments. It may be an opening up of your spare-time prospects. Or it may come from something outside any of these. *But because of the psychic tension you have built up in your practices for the Creation of Prosperity, something there must be.*

TAKING CONTROL

You don't however need to wait passively for it like a thirsty field awaiting a rainstorm. And you don't need to 'push the wheels around' at the earthly level. That is not the way. **In the Creation of Prosperity there are psychic processes at work – and there are powerful psychic methods to step up those processes.**

In utilizing these methods you will be controlling and directing the potential for **expansion** and **opportunity** which is being generated by your magnetic field of PROSPERITY and INCREASE, and thereby effectively establishing the foundation for your work as an ADVANCED CREATOR OF PROSPERITY. The first step here is to develop a working relationship with your own **Deep Mind**.

FUNCTIONS OF THE DEEP MIND

Your rational mind is your conscious, knowing mind. It is in control of your voluntary actions, such as speaking or crossing the road. Indispensable though it is, it covers only a small proportion of the activity of your psyche, that is to say, of the whole non-material area of your psyche.

Your Deep Mind is that part of your psyche which is called 'subconscious' by some psychologists and 'unconscious' by others. Not that it is unconscious in itself, but that the rational mind is unconscious of it and has no direct access to its activities. Its levels and modes of action are manifold, and its powers are still to some extent – probably to a very great extent – unexplored.

One level of your Deep Mind works with the autonomic nervous systems and controls for example your digestion, or 'involuntary' actions such as sneezing or coughing.

You may wonder whether 'mind' is really involved in such happenings. But you probably know how worry can affect the digestion. Again, notice people coughing when they listen to a dull speaker. They 'can't help it'. If the speaker brightens up and recaptures their interest, however, the coughing dies down at once!

Your Deep Mind can also take control, briefly, of what should be voluntary actions such as speech. It can play odd tricks in this way.

'I cooked this without using a recipe', says your hostess proudly.

'Yes, I guessed that', you hear yourself saying in the warm, appreciative tone you had ready to make a more polite comment.

Incidents of this sort are funny or embarrassing, but they show how essential it is not to let your Deep Mind take control of things. Of itself it is unpredictable and disconcertingly outspoken, very much like a child.

PUCK AND ARIEL

If you know your Shakespeare – and the plays can be good friends to the Creator of Prosperity – you can find matter for thought by regarding these two characters as different illustrations of the Deep Mind: **Puck** in *A Midsummer*

Night's Dream and **Ariel** in *The Tempest*.

Seen in this way, Puck can be taken to represent the Deep Mind dominant, playing boisterous pranks on people who have no notion how to take control of the situation. Their responses of bewilderment and fear only build up further the despotism of the unruly sprite.

Ariel on the other hand will represent the Deep Mind controlled by a master character, the wise mage Prospero. Treated with genuine love but firm command, Ariel delights to exercise his unearthly abilities in assisting Prospero's works of high power.

*It is precisely the **Prospero-Ariel** type of relationship that you are going to establish with your Deep Mind!*

THE SUBLIMINAL PORTAL

A special tool must now be introduced into your Creation of Prosperity practices. This is the BLACK MIRROR, an instrument that has been used for centuries in connection with visualization practices, specialized forms of divination, and techniques of creative psychism.

Various forms of the Black Mirror have been employed through the ages: some elaborate, others less so. For the Creator of Prosperity the following simple options are recommended:

PREPARING THE BLACK MIRROR

1 – **A rectangle of wood, stiff card or other rigid material**, approximately 30 cm x 22 cm. The front of this is painted a *glossy* black, and the rectangle provided with

means of standing freely upon a flat surface.

2 – **A ready-made free-standing mirror, oval or rectangular in shape**, approximately 30 cm tall and 22 cm across at its greatest width, with the glass painted a *glossy* black.

For use, arrange the Black Mirror so that when you are seated before it you will be able to discern therein, more or less distinctly, your shadowy, reflected head-and-shoulders image. *Don't worry! You really don't want a clear reflection.*

Your Mirror is to serve as a gateway between levels of awareness, whereby you will open communication with your Deep Mind and enlist its potent help in your programme for the Creation of Prosperity. The Mirror is special, so it should be treated with respect and never used for any other purpose, and when it is not being used, it should be kept covered with a white veil.

A VITAL ALLIANCE

It's important to understand *why* you can do what will do next.

Your Deep Mind is in every sense 'profound'. It is the deepest and most powerful part of what is called your 'lower nature' – which comprises, besides your Deep Mind, your instincts, emotions and of course your physical body. It is, furthermore, your indispensable power source for all psychic action.

The rational mind is often adjudged to be part of the 'lower nature'. If it follows the guidance of sense perceptions, instincts and emotions, that judgment of it is true. But when your rational mind invokes and allies itself with the high spiritual forces of the cosmos, it is no longer a part of your 'lower nature' but becomes in truth the 'godlike intellect' of which the older poets and philosophers speak.

In the Creation of Prosperity this vital alliance of rational mind with spiritual force is achieved through regular use of the 'Dwelling in the Creative Light' technique. Here, the rational mind, continually receptive to and inspired by the cosmic forces of Abundance, is properly able to direct the Deep Mind with kindly authority. To direct it, moreover, with a singular and specific dynamism, for the achievement of Prosperity and Increase.

GETTING ACQUAINTED

In the following procedure, your image, since it reflects a part of your 'lower nature' – your physical body and emotional expression – and is a valid symbol of your unconscious, is altogether suitable to represent your Deep Mind. It is to be understood as representative of ARIEL; and you, PROSPERO, whose rational mind is attuned to the forces of Abundance, are going to secure its co-operation.

BASIC MIRROR TECHNIQUE

Preparation

1 – When you are alone and relaxed, set up your Mirror, covered with its white veil, upon a table.

2 – Be sure that whatever light source you employ shines upon you from behind the Mirror or above it. You need to be able to discern your reflection in the Mirror, but you do not want to cast your shadow upon it.

3 – *If it helps you in creating a relaxed and 'psychic' atmosphere, light two candles, one at each side and slightly to the rear of your Mirror.*

4 – *If you wish, burn some of your favourite incense.*

Practice

1 – Standing before the Mirror, perform the 'Dwelling in the Creative Light' technique. *Do not proceed at once to step 8 of this technique, however, but remain in step 7 while you say:*

THE LIGHT OF ABUNDANCE SURROUNDS ME

THE POWER OF ABUNDANCE SUSTAINS ME

THE VITALITY OF ABUNDANCE INSPIRES MY DOINGS

Pause briefly for reflection upon your words, then continue:

I AM ONE WITH THE FORCES OF ABUNDANCE

Again, pause briefly for reflection, then continue:

AND BY THE LIGHT OF MY HIGHER SELF

I CALL UPON MY DEEP MIND TO ASSIST ME

IN ACHIEVING PROSPERITY AND INCREASE

FOR THE GOOD OF MY ENTIRE BEING

2 – Complete step 8 of 'Dwelling in the Creative Light', allowing the formulations to fade from your consciousness, and opening your eyes.

3 – Seat yourself before the Mirror, and with your right hand

tap gently three times upon it. Then, with both hands, remove and set aside the veil.

4 - Hold your hands palms uppermost before you, with forearms resting upon the table.

Now look into the Mirror.

Consider the Ariel aspect of your Deep Mind, represented here by your mysterious reflection. It is an elfin child. It possesses amazing powers, yet it is dependent for its ultimate wellbeing upon your right guidance. As dependent as you (your conscious, rational self) are upon your link with, and your receptivity to, the spiritual forces of light and life that emanate from your higher self.

5 – Engage the attention of your Deep Mind gently. Begin by giving it a friendly greeting, such as: **'Hello, my Deep Mind. Come out of your dreams for a while. I know you are in there and I want to talk to you'**.

6 – Close your eyes and say, **'I'm *Frankie Roe'*** *(use whatever name you like best to be called),* then open your eyes and say, **'and you're my Deep Mind, my good friend and ally'**.

7 – Exchange a big smile with your Deep Mind. Tell it of your love for it *(you may well have neglected it in the past)*, of your genuine concern for its well-being, and of your confidence in its power to help you.

8 – Tell your Deep Mind, in your own way, of your desire to be a successful Creator of Prosperity. Ask it to help you in your aims to increase and direct the currents of Abundance for your mutual benefit; but don't yet make any specific request. *Remember you are addressing an immensely powerful, innocent and willing aspect of your psyche, and the*

relationship is at an early stage.

9 – Close your eyes, and visualize once again the shining sphere of white light just above but not touching your head. Holding this image in mind, mentally affirm your intention to achieve Prosperity and Increase for the good of your entire being.

10 – Now open your eyes, and still holding the shining sphere in your visual imagination, raise both hands in blessing, with palms towards the Mirror, and say:

MY DEEP MIND

MY SPECIAL FRIEND AND HELPER

I THANK YOU FOR ASSISTING ME

MAY THE BLESSINGS OF PROSPERITY AND INCREASE

BE YOURS IN THEIR FULLNESS

AS WE ADVANCE IN THE LIGHT OF ABUNDANCE

11 – Let the sphere of light fade from your awareness. Finally, veil the Mirror, then clap your hands three times to dispel your meditative mood and to affirm your return to every day consciousness.

THE ONWARD VIEW

In establishing a firm relationship with your Deep Mind, *routine* and *habit* are of great value because, by their very nature, they form the connecting link between conscious thought and spontaneous action.

One way you can establish *routine* and *habit* is by performing the Mirror practice always at the same time of day so far as you can. And have a particular way of tapping upon the Mirror – it's a special signal to a friend.

Another important factor is that you should keep the practice up daily – again, so far as you can. You should continue with the 'Basic Mirror Technique', in the form in which it is given, until you feel your relationship with your Deep Mind is firmly established and you are therefore ready to extend or embellish the technique or go on to further procedures.

Only you yourself can be the judge of this readiness, so you need to watch how the relationship is developing. But if as you progress you feel from time to time a need to alter somewhat the words you address to Ariel – even the words of the closing speech of thanks in step 9 – then you *should* alter them. This is part of your progress from a formal introduction to a meaningful personal relationship.

6

MONITORING THE DEEPS

Like any personality of youth and brilliance, Ariel sparkles increasingly in response to a greater measure of notice and appreciation. By opening another window – so to put it – upon Ariel's activities in addition to your work with the Black Mirror, you will not only be enabled to monitor the progress of the Mirror work, you will be able at the same time to stimulate that progress and in fact to advance your whole relationship with your Deep Mind.

OPENING THE WINDOW

If you have not given much attention before to your dreams, you may think there will be difficulties about this. Perhaps you are not often consciously aware of dreaming at all. Perhaps the dreams you recall seem to be mere reflections of part of the previous day's happenings. Or you may remember only dreams which appear to you pure fantasy, not related to your personal life at all. Or your dreams may seem to be a chaotic medley of unrelated fragments.

No matter how you dream – and every dreamer has an individual *style* – your dreams will begin to develop coherence and clarity when you give them ATTENTION.

It may take a little time. A person who 'never dreams' might need to give a few weeks of attention to the subliminal levels of the psyche before getting a dream that remains in some measure accessible to the rational mind when the sleeper awakes. But then communication with the Deep Mind is likely to come in a rush. Whether you need to use as much patience as that or whether the dreams – understood or not – come easily, **take the first important step at once, and note them down in a Dream Diary.**

Write each dream down as soon as possible after waking. Details often fade quickly, and details can often give important clues as to what the dream area of your Deep Mind is telling you. If you can't put a dream on paper at once, record it on tape until you can write it. If you feel a dream would gain by being illustrated, add a sketch if you can, or cut and paste in magazine pictures that give the feeling of the dream.

When you've begun collecting your dreams in this way, see if you can get the general drift of what they are saying.

DREAM WATCHING

There are some simple rules in dream watching which will help you, and which will also encourage your Deep Mind to communicate with you.

1 – Never leave a dream out of your record because it is incomplete or because it seems too weird. It may make

more sense when you look at it again, even if only after a few days.

2 – Realize that your Deep Mind mostly 'talks in pictures' in the dream state. It may take bits and pieces from anything you've ever seen, heard or experienced, in much the same way as you can do with those magazine clippings: to give the *feeling* of its message, or occasionally an important keyword, either straight or as a sort of simple charade.

3 – Realize, also, that your Deep Mind is not trying to set puzzles for you, and neither is it trying to *hide* its meanings from you. Don't weave up clever 'interpretations' of your dreams. Note particularly how a dream 'feels' – happy, sad, anxious or whatever – and what the action suggests to you. SIMPLICITY is the secret of success in understanding your Deep Mind.

4 – Don't share your dreams with anyone, not even with your closest friend. Of course in the general way of things, people compare notes about their dreams as a matter of ordinary conversation, and there's no harm done. But you are carefully building up a special relationship with your Deep Mind (and, ultimately, for a very special purpose), and no other person can possibly understand your Deep Mind's 'language' as you can.

POINTERS TO PROGRESS

Dream watching becomes a fascinating business, and through it you will learn a lot about yourself and about your inner life. But that is not your only motive in watching your dreams. Almost at once, you'll probably find that as you begin taking note of your dreams, your work with the Mirror takes on enhanced vitality. This advance will also take effect in your dream life.

Your dreams will doubtless go on relating to all kinds of subject matter, but in them you will find, at first on a few 'big' occasions, but then more frequently, a new, friendly figure: **a person who is a good companion, willing and able to solve problems or help you out of difficulties.** You may or may not in your dream identify this person with ARIEL, but it is in fact a representation of that aspect of your Deep Mind. *The appearance of this figure is an important sign of the establishment of the relationship you are seeking.* Again, you may dream of the Black Mirror itself, either in its own form or in some other. In the early stages it might seem to be a mysterious curtain between yourself and your friend, but as you progress it may appear as a doorway. Consider how you feel about it in your dream: are you concerned, are you confident, are you hopeful? Or do you just go through it, or welcome your friend through it, without any strangeness at all? It may be that through this doorway you see other people, scenes, activity. It may be that you develop a heightened awareness of the world of the psyche, that you get premonitions whether in dream or awake, that you observe coincidences which seem more than coincidences. Any of these things are good pointers to progress for you. *Your relationship and dialogue with the Ariel-aspect of your Deep Mind are bearing fruit.*

Dream Watching provides an exciting way to monitor your progress in the basic Mirror practice. But its usefulness doesn't end there. As a means of exploring the state of your relationship with your Deep Mind, of enhancing 'dialogue' and receiving 'advice' from Ariel, it will be of value to you as you embark upon the more advanced techniques for the Creation of Prosperity. In Addendum B you will find a **Catalogue of Dream Symbols**. This is provided not only to assist you in 'interpreting' the promptings of your unconscious in relation to the basic Mirror practice, but as on ongoing key to the dreams which your work as an Advanced Creator of Prosperity will engender.

7

YOUR TALENTS

Talents are generally thought of in three groups, although the divisions are vague and there is naturally a lot of overlapping. But people often refer to **practical**, **artistic** or **psychic** talents.

You probably know of your practical talents. They may be talents for car maintenance, DIY jobs, growing vegetables, doing the family accounts, anything of an obviously useful and 'practical' nature. Even so, it happens sometimes that an emergency calls forth an unsuspected practical talent in a person, and he or she surprises everyone by coping efficiently with something never before attempted.

BURIED TALENTS

Artistic and psychic talents are more often buried, either because they were deliberately set aside in early life, or because it never occurred to anyone – least of all to the owner – that they might be there. Many people have in this way unsuspected talents for painting, writing, dress design, music, drama, dance – any one of a multitude of art forms. As for psychic talents, people who know themselves to be clairvoyant or telepathic, or to possess powers of prediction, frequently don't care to admit the fact even to themselves. These talents are as a rule regarded with disfavour as being the reverse of 'practical'. They can however belong to very practical people, and can be put to very practical use: a good example of the 'overlapping' of categories referred to above.

SEARCHING FOR THE LODE

The techniques you are using for the Creation of Prosperity will already have enhanced your natural psychic faculties. Now you are deliberately going to increase the general potency of your psychic energies, and then direct and develop them in advanced techniques for Creating Prosperity and Creative Investment.

In this, you will be opening further doors between the levels within yourself, improving the flow of communication with your Deep Mind and adding a new dimension of power to your programme, for the sure achievement of Greater Prosperity and Increase.

Use of the following techniques – even though they are designed to inculcate a *general* development of your psychic powers – are likely to bring to the fore a specific psychic talent, whether this be clairvoyance, clairaudience, precognition or the like. At the same time, your Deep Mind will not miss the point of the exercise and will support the central dynamism of your work as a Creator of Prosperity by developing precisely those psychic talents which are fundamental to your intention and success.

INCREASING PSYCHIC ENERGY

Preparation

1 – Last thing at night, when you are alone and relaxed, set up your Mirror, covered with its white veil, upon a table.

2 – Be sure that the light source you employ is suitably arranged.

3 – If you wish, light two candles, one at each side and slightly to the rear of your Mirror.

4 – Burn incense, if you so desire.

Practice Part 1

1 – Standing before the Mirror, perform the 'Dwelling in the Creative Light' technique. *Do not proceed at once to step 8 of this technique, however, but remain in step 7 while you say:*

THE LIGHT OF ABUNDANCE SURROUNDS ME

THE POWER OF ABUNDANCE SUSTAINS ME

THE VITALITY OF ABUNDANCE INSPIRES MY DOINGS

Pause briefly for reflection upon your words, then continue:

I AM ONE WITH THE FORCES OF ABUNDANCE

Again, pause briefly for reflection, then continue:

AND BY THE LIGHT OF MY HIGHER SELF

I CALL UPON MY DEEP MIND TO ASSIST ME

IN ACHIEVING PROSPERITY AND INCREASE

FOR THE GOOD OF MY ENTIRE BEING

2 – Complete step 8 of 'Dwelling in the Creative Light', allowing the formulations to fade from your consciousness, and opening your eyes.

3 – Seat yourself before the Mirror, and with your right hand tap gently three times upon it. Then, with both hands, remove and set aside the veil.

4 - Hold your hands palms uppermost before you, with forearms resting upon the table.

Now look into the Mirror.

Consider the Ariel aspect of your Deep Mind, represented by your mysterious reflection. Give your Deep Mind a smile and a greeting, speaking gently to it in your own words.

5 -Then, still with eyes open, visualize once again the shining sphere of white light just above but not touching your head. Maintaining this visualization, raise both hands towards the Mirror, and say:

DEEP MIND

FRIEND AND HELPER

IT IS MY DESIRE TO ADVANCE UNDERSTANDING

AND TO INCREASE COMMUNICATION BETWEEN US

THAT TOGETHER WE MAY PROSPER

IN THE LIGHT OF ABUNDANCE –

POWERFULLY INCREASE MY PSYCHIC ENERGIES

AND PLACE UNDER MY DIRECTION AND CONTROL

THOSE PSYCHIC FACULTIES WHICH WILL ENABLE ME

TO SEE MORE DISTINCTLY AND BRING TO FRUITION

EVERY OPPORTUNITY FOR INCREASE

WHICH WILL BENEFIT OUR MUTUAL GOOD

IN THE CREATION OF PROSPERITY

6 – Veil the Mirror, *but do not clap your hands.*

Practice Part 2

7 – Lying in bed, relax yourself in body and mind.

8 – Think briefly *but intensely* of the Ariel aspect of your Deep Mind, then quietly say:

MY DEEP MIND

FRIEND AND HELPER

ASSIST ME IN DEVELOPING EVERY PSYCHIC FACULTY

WHICH WILL BENEFIT OUR MUTUAL GOOD

IN THE LIGHT OF ABUNDANCE

9 – Bring to mind the shining sphere of light above your head. Think only of that image until sleep comes to you.

Practice Part 3

10 – When you get up in the morning, go about your usual hygiene routine and prepare yourself, as it were, to face the world. Feel good about yourself.

11 – When you are ready, stand before the Black Mirror and perform the technique of 'Dwelling in the Creative Light'. *Do not proceed at once to step 8 of this technique, however, but remain in step 7 while you say:*

I AM ONE WITH THE LIGHT OF ABUNDANCE

AND IN THIS LIGHT

AND WITH THE HELP OF MY DEEP MIND

I WILL INCREASE MY PSYCHIC ENERGIES

TO ACHIEVE EVERY SUCCESS

IN THE CREATION OF PROSPERITY

12 – Complete step 8 of 'Dwelling in the Creative Light', allowing the formulations to fade from your consciousness, and opening your eyes.

13 – Seat yourself before the Mirror, and with your right hand tap gently three times upon it. Then, with both hands, remove and set aside the veil.

4 - Hold your hands palms uppermost before you, with forearms resting upon the table.

Now look into the Mirror.

Consider the Ariel aspect of your Deep Mind, represented by your mysterious reflection. Give your Deep Mind a smile and bid it a friendly 'Good Morning'!

15 -Then, still with eyes open, visualize once again the shining sphere of white light just above but not touching your head. Maintaining this visualization, raise both hands towards the Mirror, and say:

DEEP MIND

FRIEND AND ALLY

I THANK YOU FOR YOUR HELP THIS PAST NIGHT

CONTINUE TO STRENGTHEN MY PSYCHIC ENERGIES

AS I WORK FOR OUR MUTUAL GOOD

IN THE LIGHT OF ABUNDANCE

16 – Veil the Mirror, then clap your hands three times.

MOVEMENT AND PRANA

The Fivefold Prana Sequence can now be introduced into our work. This Prana Breathing method, with its great potency in amplifying and distributing psychic energy throughout the subtle level of your being, has other uses beyond its function in the present context. You will meet with it again in your programme.

At this point, it can be used to good effect, immediately or closely following your use of *Part 3* of the technique for 'Increasing Psychic Energy'. Your Deep Mind will know what you are doing, and your work with the Deep Mind will be significantly enhanced by this new technique.

To put the matter briefly: what oxygen is to the entire physical body as an energizer and indeed a necessity of life, so Prana is to the psychic level of being. Esoteric science in both East and West has long known and has utilized in a variety of ways the powerful link between physical breathing and the mysterious functions of the psyche.

According to those ancient and deeply revered Hindu writings, the Upanishads, Prana is the essential life-force, and is carried upon and can be directed with the breath.

Prana is perceived as the vital factor in the current of our life and in our ability for power and magnetism. Its control and employment are thus an indispensable concern for the Creator of Prosperity.

THE FIVEFOLD PRANA SEQUENCE

1 – **PRANA, 'breathing out'.**

Stand erect and relaxed.

From a normal breath, breathe out strongly and deeply. Initially let your arms hang naturally at your sides. As your lungs become emptied of air you may bend your torso forwards, flex your knees slightly and place your palms on your thighs to aid the expiration of as much air as possible. This breathing out should be completed within about twelve heartbeats. Go straight on to:

2 – **APANA, 'breathing in' or 'halted breath'.**

After a pause *of one heartbeat only* with no breath in the lungs, stand erect again and breathe in, fully and naturally.

Breathe out to a normal extent, and in again, several times to establish an unhurried, strong, rather deep breathing in a rhythm you can easily maintain. 'As if you were sleeping' is a good description. Continue this rhythm while passing on to the next step:

3 – **VYANA, 'dividing breath'.**

As you breathe out, imagine distinctly that the Prana, the vital essence carried by the air you exhale, does not go forth from your nostrils or mouth but out through the top of your head. There it divides into two streams, arching to left and right over your shoulders like a fountain, and descends to the earth (*that is, to just below the level of your feet*).

From there, as you breathe in, the two streams curve inwards to your feet and, reuniting, ascend steadily up through the midline of your body to the region of your heart and chest.

Then, as you breathe out again, the flow ascends upwards from your lungs and through your head, to divide and descend as before.

The two continuous cycles of movement – *out-breath*, with the Prana arising from your lungs, going out through the top of your head and falling to the earth; *in-breath*, with the Prana curving inwards to your feet, reuniting and ascending to your chest – comprise your whole body in their flow.

After performing the twin cycle seven times, proceed to:

4 – **UDANA, 'ascending breath'.**

Continuing to breathe rhythmically, imagine the Prana accumulating in your feet. (*You may actually feel a sensation of tingling warmth in your insteps at this stage*).

Without delay, on a deep in-breath imagine that you are drawing the gathered force up to your heart. And as you breathe out, mentally affirm:

I AM ONE WITH THE FORCES OF ABUNDANCE

Expel this same breath deeply and with force, imagining the stream of Prana ascending swiftly from the region of your heart, out through the top of your head and upwards, immeasurably upwards into the cosmos. This brings you to:

5 – *SAMANA, 'collecting breath'.*

On the next inhalation, imagine the vital essence flooding down upon you from the cosmic heights, immensely augmented in potency. It descends upon you in luminous power, sweeping through every part of your body from head to foot, vitalizing and energizing you with the life-force, its radiant joy and compelling magnetism.

Continue to breathe steadily and rhythmically as you return to ordinary awareness.

THE CENTRAL DYNAMISM

Enhancement and direction of your psychic potential is not, in this programme, dependent upon routine exercises but upon *the actual intention and enactment of your work as a* **Creator of Prosperity**. Your Deep Mind is aware of this, and will follow your lead, for the true attainment of Prosperity and Increase, in accord with the central dynamism of your work – *Creation of Prosperity in the Light of Abundance, for the good of your entire being.*

Having 'set the wheels in motion' at subliminal level your

task is, indeed, to provide the vehicle for actualization of your potential in *the real world,* to channel and implement your energies through positive action. At the same time, be prepared for interesting dreams. Be prepared also that the current stage of your work may reveal to your consciousness viable mundane talents.

You may dream you are doing the particular thing you have a talent for, painting or swimming or whatever. You may dream you are observing something related to the talent, like listening to music you can afterwards remember and play. Or the dream may give you a sample of the talent itself, such as the art of dreaming true.

TIME, EVENTS AND YOUR DEEP MIND

If you have dreams which foretell future events. Or which show you current events which are happening at a distance from you, don't be discouraged if at first they are mixed with seemingly unrelated dream-stuff. What your conscious mind sees as irrelevant may be included for good purpose by your Deep Mind.

When your Deep Mind draws the images it needs from the great 'scrapbook' of your life experiences like a child constructing something in play, it is concerned only with obtaining the effect it needs. The associations attached to that particular fragment by your conscious mind may not have much to do with the basic emotional 'colours and forms' seen therein by your Deep Mind. Certainly, too, the labels of past, present and future have little significance in the matter.

Quite definitely, your Deep Mind can perceive future happenings.

If the Ariel aspect of your Deep Mind knows that prophetic material is what you want, this will be brought into your dreaming. It will at first, however, until more practice is gained, be likely for example to highlight the joyfulness of the future occasion with an incident from your cousin's wedding last summer, or to provide an episode whose conclusion is still in the lap of the gods with an ending out of a recent soap.

Such happenings could shake your confidence in the real prophetic qualities of your dreaming, although they ought not to do so. This is a special reason why you need to get the dream as accurately as possible on paper, then reflect on it and sift out, at leisure, as many bits and pieces as you can attribute to known origins. Some of the built-in fragments may be collected from years back and from all kinds of sources, so don't try to rush it. When you are ready, it will be a good thing if you can spare the time to list out these 'plagiarisms' in your dream, after recording the dream itself in your diary. What you are left with should be the prophetic material in a relatively pure state.

Note this also. If the prophetic part of the dream is partly fulfilled, say a week later, don't jump to the conclusion that the rest of the 'prophecy is nonsense'.

Your Deep Mind, you'll have gathered, has little sense of time. Having brought into dream consciousness one future event, it can thereby have been made aware of another, more distant future event, and have packaged them together for you.

In a profound sense your Deep Mind is doing the spade work in regard to uncovering your talents: your task is to record, and to utilize, the findings in your ongoing programme.

8

INFUSING THE IMAGE (1)

When your Deep Mind understands what you want of it, it will either help you achieve success in your own manner or surprise you by achieving the result in some quite unexpected way.

Usually if the Deep Mind is to help you in some project, it is best if you don't dictate or even suggest *how* the purpose is to be achieved. Only, be firm and definite as to what you want.

ONE THING AT A TIME

Perhaps you want new business contacts or a new car, better business premises, a more advanced computer or, quite simply, extra money to help you achieve a vital objective.

Whatever your desire, be sure that you really *need* the thing for which you are going to ask. A frivolous or unnecessary desire is not likely to engage either the full attention or the co-operation of your Deep Mind.

You can ask the help of Ariel on *one* particular matter. It can be as great a matter as you like, but keep it simple. *Plan the statement of your need beforehand*, but don't be like the man whose one 'simple' requirement was to live to see clearly his great-grandson eating from golden plates, to the distinctly audible sound of beautiful music.

If you have a series of desires, plan to gain them one at a time.

INFUSING THE IMAGE – 1
(*RECEIVING BLESSING IN THE LIGHT OF ABUNDANCE*)

Preparation

1 – When you are alone and relaxed, set up your Mirror, covered with its white veil, upon a table.

2 – Be sure that the light source you employ is suitably arranged.

3 – If you wish, light two candles, one at each side and slightly to the rear of your Mirror.

4 – Burn incense, if you so desire.

Practice

1 – Standing before the Mirror, perform the 'Dwelling in the Creative Light' technique. *Do not proceed at once to step 8 of the technique, however, but remain in step 7 while you say:*

THE LIGHT OF ABUNDANCE SURROUNDS ME

THE POWER OF ABUNDANCE SUSTAINS ME

THE VITALITY OF ABUNDANCE INSPIRES MY DOINGS

Pause briefly for reflection upon your words, then continue:

I AM ONE WITH THE FORCES OF ABUNDANCE

Again, pause briefly for reflection, then continue:

AND BY THE LIGHT OF MY HIGHER SELF

I CALL UPON MY DEEP MIND TO ASSIST ME

IN ACHIEVING PROSPERITY AND INCREASE

FOR THE GOOD OF MY ENTIRE BEING

2 – Complete step 8 of 'Dwelling in the Creative Light', allowing the formulations to fade from your consciousness, and opening your eyes.

3 – Seat yourself before the Mirror, and with your right hand tap gently three times upon it. Then, with both hands, remove and set aside the veil.

4 - Hold your hands palms uppermost before you, with forearms resting upon the table.

Look into the Mirror.

Turn your attention to your Deep Mind, represented by your mysterious reflection in the Mirror. *Any greeting you give at this time should be **silent**.*

CREATIVE MONEYMAKING

5 – Now, aloud, tell your Deep Mind of your love for it and of your confidence in its powers; then tell your Deep Mind of *one thing* you wish to attain, and ask it to help you achieve this objective.

6 – Close your eyes. Let your consciousness dwell reflectively for a while upon the thing you require. Imagine it as clearly as possible, so as to 'show the picture' to your Deep Mind. Think of the benefit this thing is going to bring into your life, and of its importance in your Creation of Prosperity programme. This is something you really *need* for the further achievement of Prosperity and Increase.

7 – Still with your eyes closed, mentally 'savour' the object of your desire. If it is a car, imagine the exhilaration of driving it. If it is money, see yourself counting it and feeling its texture. See yourself shaking hands with a new business contact, and feel a warm glow of certainty about the good prospects involved. See yourself holding a well-earned cheque, and feel the sense of pride and added prosperity of the occasion. Or see yourself seated at your new computer, and feel the excitement of its potential. Whatever it is you are seeking, *imagine* and *savour* it as best fits the case.

8 – Open your eyes. Take the Mirror with both hands and bring it slightly towards you. Continuing to hold the Mirror, be aware of the Ariel aspect of your Deep Mind as represented by your reflection, and say:

DEEP MIND

MY POWERFUL FRIEND AND ALLY

I TRULY DESIRE AND NEED [name your desire]

ASSIST ME TO ACHIEVE THIS SWIFTLY AND SURELY

FOR OUR MUTUAL GOOD

AND FOR INCREASE OF BLESSING

IN THE LIGHT OF ABUNDANCE

9 - Still holding the Mirror, close your eyes. Now imagine the object of your desire appearing in the Mirror. There should be no emotional 'tone' to this: you are simply picturing 'the ideal business contact', 'the new computer', or *whatever*.

10 – Maintaining awareness of the object of your desire, as you have imagined it in the Mirror, visualize once again the shining sphere of white light just above but not touching your head. 'See' the sphere increasing in brightness until it is an effulgent glory that encompasses the Mirror-image of your desire.

Then 'see' the object of your desire glowing with light and vitality in response to the splendour of the sphere of light. Holding this formulation clearly in mind – the effulgent sphere above your head and the luminous Mirror-image – say:

THIS THING SHALL COME TO PASS

IN THE LIGHT OF ABUNDANCE

11 – Allowing the formulations to fade, open your eyes and clap your hands three times.

12 – Finally, standing before the Mirror, perform the Fivefold Prana Sequence, to circulate throughout your being the energies you have awakened and to align yourself once more with the cosmic Forces of Abundance.

A WORD

This technique is yours to use at any stage of your Prosperity programme henceforth.

When working for the achievement of a specific desire by this method, continue with the practice until your objective is realized, but do not employ the technique more than three times in a week: do not, in fact, 'nag' your Deep Mind.

Likewise, while you are using the technique for a specific acquisition, do not, *save in a case of absolute necessity*, seek to achieve a further desire by this method until the current one has been realized. Build step-by-step, to avoid dissipating your psychic energies and to maintain a clear and simple working relationship with your Deep Mind.

FREEDOM AND CONTROL

Your Deep Mind can give you its most effective help when it acts under the DIRECTION of your rational consciousness but without its INTERFERENCE.

It's like freewheeling on a bicycle: the wheels have their liberty to spin along, carrying you at speed, but still you are keeping steady control of the whole machine. It's also like the work of an expert touch typist. The typist's swift and accurate fingers would probably stumble if the conscious mind concerned itself with their action or with the subject matter of the typing. Quite likely at the end of the day, the typist could tell you nothing of what had been typed, but would know exactly what margin had been set and what spacing had been used.

So it is with the Deep Mind. You give it directions, and set it free like a carrier pigeon to perform its task in its own way.

LEARN TO LET GO

All this is very significant for you, and not only to help you perform the practices given. It's significant for the psychic action you need for *all* your activities as a Creator of Prosperity. YOU MUST LEARN TO LET GO.

Your Deep Mind can't do its best if your conscious emotions are breathing down its neck.

But how do you cope with this problem: a problem which is notorious for its tendency to inhibit psychic action?

Suppose as an example that you want to use a Mirror technique to obtain a sum of money. Suppose you need the money urgently for some serious purpose. If you are deeply worried about the matter, how can you avoid being distracted from your meditative state by this worry and this urgency?

As a Creator of Prosperity, you should not be likely ever to get into so dire a situation. But the answer to this example will help to emphasize what should be your viewpoint in money-making activities.

COPING WITH STRESS

Stress, anxiety, has both a physical and an emotional angle. The physical angle needs to be dealt with first, because it is in any case the more accessible, and also because it holds a valuable key to the emotional angle.

Any professional actor could tell you, if you keep behaving like a particular character you'll grow into feeling like that character. So, if you have a genuine cause for concern, you'll do neither yourself nor the situation any manner of good if

CREATIVE MONEYMAKING

you pace up and down, wring your hands, or otherwise act like a person overcome with worry. You need, instead, to take a positive approach.

There are a few pointers on the emotional side which are useful in any crisis situation. Give thought to them, because they need to be to some extent familiar if you are to remember them when needed:

1 – However strongly you feel about the objective situation, avoid being sorry for yourself. Self pity is altogether destructive, and you need to be CREATIVE.

2 – Don't feel guilty, either. You don't 'owe it' to yourself or anyone to entertain anxious feelings which paralyze your power to act usefully.

3 – Know you are strong, not helpless. Something is within your power to do, and you are doing it.

4 – Perform the Fivefold Prana Sequence often, for added energy.

5 – Remember, your highest self is always with you in the fullness of its reality - even if you are unaware of its serene presence and vital action – and its powers of life and inspiration flood ceaselessly into the higher levels of your psyche. So from time to time, as you feel the need, bring to mind the luminous image which symbolises the reality of this presence in your psyche: the shining sphere of light, which you visualize just above your head.

6 – Relax.

This last point, relaxation, is as vital as the others. The relaxation needs to be physical as well as emotional.
If you are faced with an ongoing stress situation, or if you

are concerned about over-reacting, make sure you are getting all the vitamins, and iron or other minerals, you may need.

The inner attitude you require is to accept the reality of your emotions about the situation, then put them aside from your intended course of action. Your physical routine of relaxation, 'Establishing Tranquility,' will help in this.

Sometimes people say, 'Nothing succeeds like success'. This adage can be true. The successful person has the capital with which to expand his or her interests. More importantly, the successful person can easily survey the field of activity in as relaxed manner.

It doesn't always work out that way. Sometimes a successful person will get too keyed up, 'intoxicated with success', will become conceited, careless.

The Ancient Greeks recognized that dangerous state of euphoria and had a word for it: *hubris*. They showed it in many of their great dramas as the pride that goes before a fall.

It isn't only in an emergency that you need to stay relaxed. Whatever happens, even in the Wheel of Fortune sends you to the very top, *stay relaxed.* NOTHING SUCCEEDS LIKE RELAXATION. IT LETS YOU *FREEWHEEL* YOUR DEEP MIND.

9

INFUSING THE IMAGE (2)

Hundreds upon hundreds of good causes are appealing all the time. Of course, you don't have any bounden duty to help them. Maybe you don't feel you can truly afford to give. But are you entitled to ignore them? Or if you give money, do your donations help anyone as much as they set you back? Yet, beyond doubt, giving – whether you give money or otherwise – is a good thing. You benefit directly those to whom you give. Also, by keeping the currents of prosperity and the interchange of life-forces circulating, you benefit society at large. And as you are a member of society, you also benefit yourself again.

PROSPERITY IS A TWO-WAY CURRENT

These are trite and familiar truths. But you as a Creator of Prosperity can go far beyond even that circulating of the forces of Abundance. You can do far more good for your chosen cause or causes, and far more also for yourself, because you are able to activate and bring into play the high and powerful forces of Prosperity and Increase. You are not asked to risk killing your golden goose, or the magnetism of your nest egg. If you give something on the material level, that's fine. **But it will only be a token, a shadow of what you are able to do by other means.** And what you do beyond the material level will shower greater abundance on you too.

CHOOSE YOUR SPHERE OF ACTION

Because of your intended action beyond the material level your programme of giving becomes an intimate part of your personal life. It needs to be a matter of vital concern to you.

Here's a possible guideline for making your choice. You may have a deep wish – many people have – to do something for which you have no possible opportunity, perhaps even no adequate talent. *Practically everyone has some very real facet of their personality which simply doesn't fit in with the pattern of their life.*

There are quiet folk whose heart leaps at the sound of military music. There are avid readers of sea stories who never have seen the sea, and people in high-rise apartments whose lives can never feel complete without horses. There are lonely men as well as women whose hearts yearn for a partner and children, but whose life-style makes this an impossible dream.

So if you have unfulfilled possibilities or affinities, you are by no means alone.

But you can do something positive and creative – richly creative – about all this.

First, then, choose a good cause you will help. Choose two, if your inward affinities are completely divergent. But don't multiply your choices. To avoid diffusing your mental and emotional powers, spreading them too thin, is as important as avoiding scattering your monetary resources.

Keep to the one or two causes which matter vitally to *you*. Other people will certainly act upon this principle, but their choices will differ from yours. So from their diversity every kind of good cause receives attention, and you need not feel guilty because of some worthy cause which is just 'not you'.

REFINING THE CHOICE

There are organizations which care for children, for old people, for disabled war veterans, for victims of particular calamities – earthquakes, volcanic eruptions, floods, hurricanes, invasions, famine. Some specialize in the problems of a particular country.

There are rescue associations trained and equipped for valiant work at sea, on the mountains, in wilderness or wreckage. There are causes concerned with specific objectives of medical research. There are religious groups, teaching, nursing, handing on the traditions of their faith. There are historical preservation and publication societies, archaeological groups for rediscovering the past. There are organizations to help young artists of every kind to follow their chosen calling.

There are those whose work it is to help the plight of domesticated animals who have become totally dependent on the goodwill of humankind. There are those who study and seek to better the lot of wild creatures – mammals, birds, marine life; and there are those who work for the preservation of the forests and for the biosphere as a whole, upon which all life depends.

Choose, therefore, according to those deep impulses of your own nature whose lack of fulfillment is a matter of vital concern to you. That way, by what you give – at the material or other level – you will be helping others and at the same time finding a more complete self-expression than the circumstances of your life would otherwise allow.

BEYOND MATERIAL DONATIONS

As a Creator of Prosperity, however, you cannot adequately express your sincere concern for a chosen cause by merely material means. Your powers of material giving are limited, but you know that you have at your disposal the great forces of Prosperity and Increase far beyond your own earthly means.

You can give an inestimable amount to this concern which is vital to you, and the first step is to make it truly a part of your life.

Each of the numberless charitable organizations, and the cause for which it works, opens up to anyone who is involved an endless vista of interest. Some of them provide publications about their work. But in any case you should find out all you can about the activity, and the background to the activity, of your own particular cause.

BE ALIVE TO THOSE WHO CONCERN YOU

If you are helping children, you'll want to know about their health problems or their vocational prospects. The same for old people. Maybe they do craftwork for which you can help find a market? Find out what campaigns your veterans fought in, what medals they won. Old soldiers don't like to see themselves regarded simply as objects of compassion. They like to know you appreciate and remember what they did. The same with members of the rescue teams. They can certainly use funds, but they like their skillful and often perilous work to be known and appreciated also.

It's the same with any of the other organizations you may choose. Let them know you have a real interest in their work. Those that care for animals, or for the environment, usually have newsletters or other communications to which you can subscribe. But go deeper, read and find out all you can. This applies, whatever cause you have taken up. Who knows? – you may one day come up with an inspiration that will save them money, or improve their equipment or methods, and so give them more, in a very real way, than any donation you could make.

GIVING AND RECEIVING

The technique which follows, 'Infusing the Image – 2', is the counterpart of 'Infusing the Image – 1'. Both techniques are essential parts of the process of CIRCULATION.

This circulation, this giving and receiving, are needful for the multiplication of resources.

The returning bounty you receive will be far greater than that which you sent forth. That is *the natural principle of Increase,* applied with your knowledge of the power of your Deep Mind and of the forces of Abundance.

This practice can be begun any time after you have started work with 'Infusing the Image – 1', and you can have this *different* Infusion program running concurrently with the other.

It is at its most powerfully effective when used for causes which are really 'part of your life'. Whether or not you have donated to a given cause makes little difference for this, although as a psychological fact you are likely to feel more committed if you have a material involvement.

INFUSING THE IMAGE – 2
(*GIVING BLESSING IN THE LIGHT OF ABUNDANCE*)

Preparation

1 – Set up your Mirror, covered with its white veil, upon your table.

2 – Be sure that the light source is suitably arranged.

3 – Two candles may be lighted, one at each side and slightly to the rear of your Mirror.

4 – Burn incense if desired.

5 – Because the cause in question is of vital interest to you, make sure to achieve a state of complete relaxation *before proceeding. If you think it necessary, use at this point the technique for 'Establishing Tranquility'.*

Practice

1 – Standing before the Mirror, perform the 'Dwelling in the Creative Light' technique. Do not proceed at once to step 8 of the technique, however, but remain in step 7 while you say:

THE LIGHT OF ABUNDANCE SURROUNDS ME

THE POWER OF ABUNDANCE SUSTAINS ME

THE VITALITY OF ABUNDANCE INSPIRES MY DOINGS

Pause briefly for reflection upon your words, then continue:

I AM ONE WITH THE FORCES OF ABUNDANCE

Again, pause briefly for reflection, then continue:

AND BY THE LIGHT OF MY HIGHER SELF

I CALL UPON MY DEEP MIND TO ASSIST ME

IN BLESSING MY CHOSEN CAUSE

FOR GREATER CIRCULATION

OF THE BENEFITS OF ABUNDANCE,

AND ENHANCEMENT OF PROSPERITY AND INCREASE

FOR THE GENERAL GOOD

AND FOR MY OWN WELL-BEING

2 – Complete step 8 of 'Dwelling in the Creative Light', allowing the formulations to fade from your consciousness, and opening your eyes.

3 – Seat yourself before the Mirror, and with your right hand tap gently three times upon it. Then, with both hands, remove and set aside the veil.

4 – Hold your hands palms uppermost before you, with forearms resting upon the table.

Look into the Mirror.

Turn your attention to your Deep Mind, represented by your mysterious reflection in the Mirror. *Any greeting you give at this time should be* **silent**.

5 – Now, aloud, tell your Deep Mind of your desire and intention to bless your specific cause in the Light of Abundance, and ask your Deep Mind to assist you in accomplishing this objective.

6 – Close your eyes. Let your consciousness dwell reflectively for a while upon your chosen cause. Let your garnered knowledge and understanding of the subject be present in your consciousness. *There is no need of haste.*

7 – When you are ready, open your eyes. Take the Mirror with both hands and bring it slightly towards you. Continuing to hold the Mirror, and being aware of the Ariel aspect of your Deep Mind, visualize once again the shining sphere of white light just above but not touching your head.

8 – Now meditatively transfer to your Deep Mind the conscious awareness you have built up of your subject, your chosen cause: do this by again dwelling reflectively upon your chosen cause but while gazing now into the Mirror.

9 – While this meditative transfer is taking place, imagine the sphere of light above your head growing brighter and yet more bright, until in your imagination its splendour encompasses the Mirror. Keep your eyes open throughout this process.

10 – Having completed this transfer of material to your Deep Mind, and remaining strongly aware of the effulgence of the sphere of light above your head, say:

I BLESS ....

IN THE NAME AND POWER OF DIVINE ABUNDANCE

THAT IT MAY FLOURISH

TO BE SPIRITUALLY STRENGTHENED

AND MATERIALLY ENRICHED

AND SO MAY I RECEIVE RENEWED BLESSING

FROM THE COSMIC STOREHOUSE

OF PROSPERITY AND INCREASE

THUS SHALL THE VITAL EXCHANGE

OF GIVING AND RECEIVING

EVER CONTINUE IN GREATER MEASURE

AND THIS SHALL COME TO PASS

11 – Allowing the formulations to fade, replace and veil the Mirror, and clap your hands three times.

12 – Finally, standing before the Mirror, perform the Fivefold Prana Sequence, to circulate throughout your being the energies you have awakened and to align yourself once more with the cosmic Forces of Abundance.

10

THE CREATIVE INVESTOR

Many people become investors simply by turning the money they've saved over to an investment corporation, or a bank, which, as one of its services, will place the money with one of various concerns to gain the best interest rates that can be had with maximum security. Such institutions generally know their job, and the investors can – and often do – cease to give the matter another thought except to take note of the moderate but regular dividends appearing on their bank statements.

There's no reason why you should not invest in this way as a beginning. But the scope and potential of your activity as a Creative Investor should go far beyond that.

YOU NEED KNOWLEDGE

Your Deep Mind will work on material which is made available to it. What your rational consciousness learns and concerns itself with will filter through to your Deep Mind which will process it in its own manner. For this reason, you should also be regularly studying one or two publications about money matters: and if you are not already doing this you should begin now.

BECOMING ACCLIMATIZED

If you are taking a first look at such a publication you may at first be horrified at the number of pages which don't interest you or even make much sense to you.

But in this, as in many things, *have patience*. A publication of this type is designed for many kinds of readers, with many different interests. There will certainly be one or more articles you can read and get involved in. Probably at first these will be on a curious diversity of topics, but no matter. What's important is that you are getting acclimatized, you are becoming consciously and unconsciously one with the money-thinking public.

FROM CONSCIOUS MIND TO DEEP MIND

From time to time, cast your eyes over lists of stocks and shares fluctuations. Some of them will begin to catch your attention. There will be articles, also, on *why* the market shifts in this or that respect.

The underlying reasons for these changes, the relationship of the money world to the larger world, should be of particular interest to you. Better than anything else probably, this will help you get the feel of the 'living' quality of the money market, its unity with the ebb and flow of affairs in the world at large. *Your imagination will respond to this, and will in turn engage your Deep Mind.*

KNOW YOUR CORPORATIONS

If your money is being invested for you, you'll want to know as much as you can about the corporations concerned and their activities. Then if you see any reference to them – either specifically by name, or their general area of production or commerce – in one of those financial journals, you can take an informed personal interest in the matter. You'll be truly involved, mentally and emotionally.

You need your Deep Mind to be stirred to join in the action, so it can be dynamically *creative*.

BLESSING YOUR INVESTMENTS

You may want to give an extra boost to the corporation in which you have your largest or most productive investments. Or some news item may seem threatening to one of them. A positive course of action is open to you.

The technique of 'Infusing the Image – 2', as has been said, has its fullest effect when used for a cause which is truly part of your life. *Your resources are also truly part of your life, and their investment is of intense personal concern to you.* You can therefore call upon the action of your Deep Mind by use of this technique, as powerfully and effectively in the case of your investments as in the case of your chosen cause.

So bless your investments by use of 'Infusing the Image – 2'. Employ the technique exactly as given in the preceding chapter, with one exception: replace the utterance of section 3 of that technique with the following:

THE LIGHT OF ABUNDANCE SURROUNDS ME

THE POWER OF ABUNDANCE SUSTAINS ME

THE VITALITY OF ABUNDANCE INSPIRES MY DOINGS

Pause briefly for reflection upon your words, then continue:

I AM ONE WITH THE FORCES OF ABUNDANCE

Again, pause briefly for reflection, then continue:

AND BY THE LIGHT OF MY HIGHER SELF

I CALL UPON MY DEEP MIND TO ASSIST ME

IN BLESSING MY CHOSEN ENTERPRISE

WHICH IS A PROMOTER OF PROSPERITY

A CONTRIBUTION TO THE GENERAL GOOD

AND A SOURCE OF INCREASE TO ME AND TO MANY

And don't forget to use the procedure for *Activating your Gain* when you receive your actual dividend or the statement thereof.

GOING *INDEPENDENT*

Because of your use of the various practices for the Creation of Prosperity, you'll find your Deep Mind working along with your rational consciousness not only swiftly but *relevantly*. Ideas which surface suddenly in the midst of your conscious thinking should not, now, be incongruous but something vitally related to the matter in hand.

A minor news item, for instance, may announce the creation of a new mobile app, or a technical process. It may have as yet only a small apparent field of application, but your Deep Mind may link it instantly with an industry you've been studying. You go on to see how this new product could transform that industry – and you realize other people besides yourself will see this. Here's your chance to 'get in on the ground floor'!

You may well decide therefore that now is the time to become an 'independent' Creative Investor.

You will most likely see no reason to disturb the holdings you have already taken through an investment corporation. They constitute an effective magnetic Nest Egg in their own right.

So you contact a stockbroker and find out what you can buy in lines that interest you.

If you want to get in on the development of a new invention or discovery, you may be too early. The shares may not be publicly available yet. But you can look to the future and discuss what possibilities will be within your range when the time comes.

Meanwhile – if you are still set on that particular venture – there's some work you can put in on it.

BESPEAKING

Naturally, you will have asked your broker to keep a lookout for these particular shares. As a Creative Investor however you'd like to be able to rely on something more than that. Your broker may well be taken up with the affairs of many other clients. Again, by the time the thing which interests you gets into production it may have changed its name several times, or it might have become a component in a much more complex product. Or you may have taken note of the inventor's name, but later he sells the rights to someone better equipped to develop and market it.

At all events, there's every reason why you should keep track of the venture psychically as well as by earthly means. A press clipping is a good 'link', particularly if you can keep the first announcement or hint you ever saw concerning this matter.

THE BESPEAKING PROCEDURE

You won't need the Black Mirror or candles on your table; but you can light incense if you like. Place the 'link' before you.

1 – Standing before the table, perform the *Fivefold Prana Sequence*. Having done this, touch the 'link' with both hands, and remaining like this, visualize just above your head the shining sphere of white light which symbolizes your highest self,

4 –See the radiance of the sphere of light increasing until it surrounds you as a luminous effulgence. Then raise your hands slightly above the 'link', palms upwards.

5 – Within the light, bring clearly to mind the invention or product the 'link' represents; then turn your palms downwards to the 'link' (but don't touch it), and say:

THIS IS FOR ME

6 – Allow the formulations to fade from awareness, and clap your hands three times to dispel your meditative mood.

THE FOLLOW-UP PROCESS

When you have completed a procedure of this kind, don't put the link away out of sight. Have it somewhere quite visible in the house, or carry it with you in your wallet or purse and look at it several times each day.

The idea is to have it where you can keep on seeing it. Sometimes you'll look at it purposely and think of what it signifies to you. Sometimes you'll see it without giving it much conscious attention, as when you are passing it on the way to the kitchen or the bathroom, for instance; or when you take out your wallet or purse to show some I.D. Those 'scarcely conscious' glimpses are the times when the clipping will most effectively jog your Deep Mind about it and about what you want.

This way, you are in no danger of becoming impatient or obsessed about the thing. It receives attention at the most creative levels, while the rest of your mind is able to deal with other matters.

It's a good example of 'freewheeling'.

TOO MANY SIGNPOSTS

Most often you will be concerned with established, well known corporations when you want to invest independently. But which?

You can sometimes seem surrounded by a mass of publicity handouts, news items, rumours, conflicting forecasts from different sources, and sincere advice which may or may not be adequately well-informed. You may wonder what counsel (if any) you should follow, and whether there is any good purpose to be achieved by adding the mandates of your own Deep Mind to the chorus of voices.

This is precisely where your own inner guidance is indispensable to you.

People with financial flair may never have heard of Creating Prosperity in the Light of Abundance. But they DON'T resolve this sort of situation by simple rational processes, although they often imagine they do.

By way of illustration, we can find parallels in two popular forms of divination.

Assuming you know very little about palmistry, did you ever pick up a book on that subject and try to use it read your own hand?

You may have discovered in yourself a flair for the subject, but chances are you found it a confusing experience. A good book on palmistry will enable you easily to identify those lines and other features which it mentions. But even those features may in your case do things which the book doesn't precisely cater for; and what about all the lines and markings on your hands which are probably not mentioned at all? Don't they mean something too?

If the writer of that book, or another talented palmist, were reading your hand there would be no such difficulty. The reader looks at any unfamiliar configuration in relation to your whole hand (and to you), considers it meditatively, and in a flash of insight 'sees' what it means.

Again, consider the importance of interpretation in astrology. Sometimes – usually out of curiosity – a person sends for an 'analysis' of their natal chart. What they receive is neither more nor less than it claims to be. Each planet is considered separately. Its position in the chart, and the personal characteristics implied by that position, are plainly set forth. The recipient may indeed feel that each planetary outline is a fair though partial portrait, but what does it all add up to? More important usually, what is the person indicated by those outlines likely to do or to experience?

A skilled astrologer could combine all these planetary positions in a diagram, consider how they related to each other and in what aspects. There would still be a great deal of data, some of it perhaps incompatible. Sometimes 'the lines cross each other', as the *I Ching* has it. But, by a spark of intuition – a 'snap judgment' the astrologer would call it – he or she would quickly have the answers to some important questions. The finer points would follow but they would not confuse the perception of the major lines of development.

THE WOOD AND THE TREES

Now the interesting thing is that palmists frequently, and astrologers more often than not, believe they do their work without 'intuition'. The insist they 'only tell you what's there'.

This, certainly, is true as far as it goes. Their knowledge and experience identifies 'what's there'. But the ability to look at the data and pounce upon the significant details – to set aside the great mass of contradictory possibilities which generally crowd each other in the greater world around each one of us – this is a true work of divination, the often unrecognized work of the Deep Mind of the seer.

This ability to see the way through the woods without being confused by the trees needs to be a work of your Deep Mind also, to open up your best path as a Creative Investor.

You should continue to absorb all you can at the rational level. Your financial journals, world news, any other source you have for the geographic, ecological and other aspects of products and processes – all this is material for the mill of your brain to grind, so it can then pass down for further action by your Deep Mind.

Absorb all you can at the rational level, but never slip into the mistake of thinking the surface process is all you are doing or all you need to do.

Beyond that, it is your Deep Mind which, to serve you well in this matter of Creative Investing, must –

> '... *look into the seeds of time
> and see which grain will grow and which will not*'

as Shakespeare, in *Macbeth*, describes the accurate scanning of the astral dimension.

INSIDE INFORMATION

You are becoming more at home with your financial journals all the time. One day as you glance down the lists of market prices, some particular item is likely to 'jump off the page' at you.

You may immediately know why, if it links up with something else you've been reading or thinking about. Or you may not have a clue, in which case it's as well to search the rest of the journal, and the general news, to discover anything you can.

But certainly, at this stage you need more information from your Deep Mind, and the following advanced Mirror Practice should now be made part of your programme.

In using this technique, you can ask your Deep Mind for news of whatever corporations or inventions genuinely interest you. As you become proficient in it, particularly in regard to 'receiving' the answers provided by your Deep Mind, you can ask two or three questions in a session; but in the early stages, while you are becoming familiar with the technique and learning to use it effectively, ask only one question at a time. Always keep your questions simple, and *plan them beforehand* so that they are concise and unambiguous.

QUESTIONING THE DEEP MIND

Preparation

1 – When you are alone and relaxed, set up your Mirror, covered with its white veil, upon a table.

2 – Be sure that the light source you employ is suitably arranged.

3 – If you wish, light two candles, one at each side and slightly to the rear of your Mirror.

4 – Burn incense, if you so desire.

Practice

1 – Standing before the Mirror, perform the 'Dwelling in the Creative Light' technique. *Do not proceed at once to step 8 of the technique, however, but remain in step 7 while you say:*

THE LIGHT OF ABUNDANCE SURROUNDS ME

THE POWER OF ABUNDANCE SUSTAINS ME

THE VITALITY OF ABUNDANCE INSPIRES MY DOINGS

Pause briefly for reflection upon your words, then continue:

I AM ONE WITH THE FORCES OF ABUNDANCE

Again, pause briefly for reflection, then continue:

AND BY THE LIGHT OF MY HIGHER SELF

I CALL UPON MY DEEP MIND TO ASSIST ME

IN THE ATTAINMENT OF KNOWLEDGE AND INSIGHT

THAT I MAY ADVANCE SECURELY AND EFFECTIVELY

IN THE WAYS OF PROSPERITY AND INCREASE

2 – Complete step 8 of 'Dwelling in the Creative Light', allowing the formulations to fade from your consciousness, and opening your eyes.

3 – Seated before the Mirror, with your right hand tap gently three times upon it. Then remove the veil.

4 – Hold your hands palms uppermost before you, with forearms resting upon the table.

Look into the Mirror.

Turn your attention to your Deep Mind, represented by your mysterious reflection in the Mirror. *Any greeting you give at this time should be **silent**.*

5 – Again close your eyes. Reflect upon the subject of your inquiry, and mentally formulate your question(s).

6 – Open your eyes. Look into the Mirror and be aware of the Ariel aspect of your Deep Mind.

7 – Out loud, tell your Deep Mind of your love for it. Speak to it of the corporation, invention, whatever, that you seek knowledge of. Tell your Deep Mind of your need for greater knowledge and insight into this area, that you may be enabled to advance in the ways of Prosperity and Increase for the good of your entire being.

8 – Now ask your question(s), and with gentle authority direct your Deep Mind to assist you with its mighty power by obtaining the required information for you.

9 – Veil the Mirror.

10 – Remaining seated, once again close your eyes. Relax. Visualize the shining sphere of light above your head, and concentrate only on this while your Deep Mind goes about its work. *Continue in peaceful contemplation of the sphere of light for about ten minutes, or until you feel inwardly impelled to resume the dialogue with your Deep Mind.*

11 – Open your eyes. Unveil the Mirror, not tapping upon it. Be aware of the Ariel aspect of your Deep Mind as represented by your mysterious reflection, and mentally repeat your question(s).

12 – Close your eyes. Remaining relaxed and breathing deeply and evenly, and still with the sphere of light held in consciousness, visualize a slender beam of white light emanating from your forehead and passing directly to the forehead of your imagined reflection.

13 – Holding these formulations clearly in mind – the radiant sphere of light above your head and the slender beam of light linking you to the Ariel aspect of your Deep

Mind – and continuing your steady breathing, sit quietly and wait for impressions to rise in your consciousness. *Your work at this stage should be entirely passive and receptive: let impressions surface gently as they will.*

14 – When you feel that the flow of material is for the time being completed, allow the beam of light to fade from your awareness, but maintain the visualization of the sphere of light as you reflect upon and analyze the material received from your Deep Mind.

15 – Open your eyes. Still holding the sphere of light in consciousness, look into the Mirror and be aware of the Ariel aspect of your Deep Mind. Say:

MY DEEP MIND

MY GOOD FRIEND AND ALLY

I THANK YOU FOR HELPING ME IN THIS WORK

CONTINUE TO AID ME

NOW AND AT ALL TIMES

THAT TOGETHER WE MAY ATTAIN

FULLNESS OF BLESSING

IN THE LIGHT OF ABUNDANCE

16 – Allow the formulations to fade from your awareness. Veil the Mirror, and clap your hands three times.

17 – To conclude this psychic process, perform the *Fivefold Prana Sequence*.

BEWARE OF THE EMOTIONAL CONTENT

The press may not always tell you, indeed the reporters may not always know, if there were moments of inward panic in the Market, or seething fury below the conciliatory surface at a political meeting. In providing you with information about the corporations which interest you your Deep Mind might, however, give an intimation of such matter to your conscious mind.

The danger is that you may misinterpret these emotions.

The don't rise up to the surface of your mind in quotation marks. Dion Fortune's Dr. Taverner remarks that if an impulse rises up in our minds we take it to be our own: and that is exactly the case with these emotions. There is no way you can be given a sample of an emotion except by feeling it. This can be very unpleasant while it lasts, and very unsettling if you allow it to be. Even a feeling of joy can be unsettling if its cause is alien to you.

If you ride these emotions, and keep yourself quite clearly and firmly aware that they are not yours, no damage will be done. You will simply have a deeper knowledge of what goes on in a sphere of activity which is of special concern to you.

AND AFTERWARDS

Practice and experience are important in 'Questioning the Deep Mind'. If you are not yet practised enough to allow all the impressions to surface swiftly, some may follow in your dreams, or during the next day. But what you asked for will be there.

Your Deep Mind will not necessarily come up with direct answers to your questions in your sleeping dreams themselves. It *may* do so. More likely, in this context, it will suggest further areas of research, further questions you should ask through the advanced Mirror practice. You should in any case take note of your dreams. Your Deep Mind will be aware of your ongoing interest and will progressively communicate more readily with your conscious mind.

Again, in the early stages, you may wake up one morning after using the Mirror practice and find the answer to your question clearly in your mind.

It may even be that several days later an answer is imparted to you casually in a lunch-time conversation – maybe with a total stranger who, on impulse, 'thought you'd be interested to know'. These things happen, particularly when the attention of the Deep Mind is involved. And, so long as they do, it really does no harm if you still feel more comfortable to call them 'coincidence'.

But with practice, the knowledge you seek will be imparted to you in ever greater clarity and completeness through the Mirror technique itself.

CLEARLY AND WITHOUT PREJUDICE

Besides dealing with matters you've consciously wanted to know about, communications from your Deep Mind can include telepathic data from near or far, subjects of aura awareness or disturbance, and psychometric or radiesthesic Impressions from objects which have come into your hands.

These subsidiary communications can be of immense value to you as an Advanced Creator of Prosperity. You need to keep the way open for them by –

1 – Staying relaxed.

2 – Taking note of your dreams.

3 – Using, from time to time, the technique for *Increasing Psychic Energy*.

As a result, you'll get these important communications clearly and *without prejudice*, just as if you were a complete newcomer to the subjects involved.

BEGINNER'S LUCK

That's what 'beginner's luck' is about. The beginner's rational mind doesn't have enough experience to interfere in the play. Neither have the beginner's emotions become deeply involved in the game.

But a beginner is not a beginner for long! That is another reason why you need your techniques for the Creation of Prosperity: to detach your Deep Mind from (let's say) the 'lost innocence' of your rational consciousness.

A FINAL WORD

Turn to account the times you live in.

Keep up to date on current affairs, current trends and developments of every sort. Your purpose is not to become a slave to the trends. You need to know them in order to master them, to see the opportunities they present.

Don't be limited by other people's views of the possibilities of the times. Your knowledge of psychic techniques and your ability to raise yourself above worry and stress should give you a great ascendancy in your life as a Creator of Prosperity. But don't let it disable you by giving you an 'ivory tower' feeling of separation from the tides of life. The work of your Deep Mind, as it goes questing for information on your behalf, will help you if there is any danger of that sort.

Take full advantage of the measureless possibilities opened up to you by the **Creation of Prosperity**: shape your future and enrich every aspect of your life.

PROSPER AND INCREASE

IN THE LIGHT OF ABUNDANCE

11

CATALOGUE OF DREAM SYMBOLS

ABYSS

A great insight, or a source of insecurity to be overcome.

ACCIDENT

To right side of body: you are prevented going (foot) or doing (hand) as you desire. *To left side of body:* you are compelled to go (foot) or to do (hand) against your desires.

ACROBAT(S)

If you are watching you need to manoeuvre in a tricky situation. *If you yourself are the acrobat* this dream may signal spontaneous attempts at astral projection.

AIRCRAFT

There is a problem you would do better not to tackle point

by point. Far better to bypass the whole thing by flying.

ANCESTOR

You are looking into the past for security, for approval or for your own inner wholeness. Take note whether in the dream you find what you seek. As a clue for positive action, think who the ancestral character is, and what he or she means to you in terms of personal development or achievement.

ANCHOR

A symbol of security and faith. Have faith in your Creation of Prosperity practices, faith in your inner powers. 'Stand firm and win through' is the meaning of this symbol.

ANGEL

A messenger of high authority – in dream, this is from the inner regions of your own being. Give special consideration to what it says, but apply your common sense also.

ANT

A model of corporate hard work. A special effort is required of you but it may not be highly rewarded.

ANTIQUES

You have a deep desire for stability, peace and a harmonious environment. To own antique objects will give you comfort on the material level, and will help you achieve the spiritual values involved.

APPLE

An important choice is before you. You should reflect before making it, knowing you have full power to choose aright. An apple is a fruit of mystery. Cut one across the middle – at right angles to the core – and you will see a five-pointed star. This star represents yourself with your five senses. It is also the star of mystery and magical power. Dialogue with your Deep Mind before making important decisions.

ARCH

A significant form of entrance. To pass through an arch in a dream indicates you are entering upon a new approach to life. If the top of the arch is rounded or not noticed, all goes easily with the new beginning. A pointed arch indicates stress, difficulty or some regret.

ARCHERY see ARROW

ARMAGEDDON

Dreams of apocalyptic symbolism have a direct and powerful reference to changes of purpose and direction *in your inner life*. If you have an intense dream of this kind, do nothing about it. It will manifest its own meaning in its own time, even though outward events will probably go on just as before.

ARROW

If you shoot an arrow, you see yourself putting creative power and energy into a new venture. If an arrow is shot at you, beware of malicious tongues.

ARTIST

To see yourself as an artist, or to admire the work of an artist, are alike dream symbols which show you have real artistic aspiration. Whatever the art form indicated, see what you can do with it.

AXE

The Double Axe comes to us from the ancient Minoan culture of Crete as a noble symbol of divine matriarchal authority.

BALLOON

You need to get away from the emotional or intellectual details of your concerns, not to escape from them but so as to take an overview of the situation.

BANNER

You need to clarify your identity, your principles, your objectives – not necessarily to the outer world, but certainly to and for yourself.

BAPTISM

To undergo in dream any ritual of this sort indicates a genuine new beginning at one level or another.

BARBED WIRE

You should not give up your good plans but an obstacle may compel you to fulfill them in a new and more patient way.

BEE

A prosperity symbol. Renowned symbol in all times of corporate hard work, resulting in rich and shared reward.

BIRD

Positive: Good and profitable news is coming to you.
Negative: Careless talk can damage your interests.

BLOOD

Positive: **A prosperity symbol.** Healthy circulation, renewal, good credit.
Negative: Waste, loss, damaged credit.

BOOK

To read: 'Knowledge is power'. Make sure you have up-to-date information on any matter relating to your Creation of Prosperity concerns. Never mind whether you get this from an actual book, video, newscast or other source.
Ledger: Check your records carefully for an unnoticed debit, an unpaid bill or any miscalculation.

BOY

An important archetypal dream-figure. Whoever you are – man or woman, junior clerk or top management – this figure represents a vital part of you. So don't take yourself too seriously – at least, not tragically and not all the time. That boy needs some play and fun, or you can't work properly.

BRIDGE

Positive: New vistas, new areas to test your talents! Go forward and explore.
Negative: Courage and care will be needed to bring you into the better prospect you hope for. But you can supply that courage and care.

BRIGANDS

As a symbol in dream, they represent a lawless part of yourself. Don't worry! – they lurk in every healthy psyche, and, like microbes which lurk in every healthy body, *they can do no harm unless they get control.* It's far better to know they are there than not to know.

BRUNETTE

If you do not associate her with a brunette you know, she may represent some person (of any physical type) to whom you show weakness because you recognize a deep-level likeness of character.

BULLION

A prosperity symbol. You are thinking big at a deep level.

CACTUS

If your dream shows one cactus as a symbol it means you. Other people may take warning from the prickles you've put out to disguise your tender heart – but don't be deceived. Your tender heart is still there. If your dream shows a cactus desert, at first sight this suggests a barren prospect. You may have feared this. But again, look deeper. The cactus manages to find water and to flourish, so you can do it.

CADUCEUS

The Staff of Hermes (Mercury), classical deity of communication and commerce. Entwined by two serpents and crowned with wings, this powerful symbol is an *image of all that makes for your success.*

CAGE

If you see yourself as being in a cage, the meaning is plain: something is temporarily halting the progress you desire. If you see some other being in a cage, only *part* of your personality is frustrated. The nature of the caged being will tell you what part of your nature it represents. Then you can plan how to get free.

CANDLE

To light a candle is always a signal – to the cosmic powers and to yourself. You are alive and active, in hope and aspiration.

CAT

Animals in general represent energies, but the cat has a particular place in dream symbolism. The cat is a guide and messenger between the levels of your own being. The black cat in particular is a manifestation of your Deep Mind and can lead you to important discoveries.
The 'lucky black cat' of tradition is very real for the Creator of Prosperity.

CATTLE

A prosperity symbol. From ancient times cattle been not only a material indicator of a person's power and prestige but also a notable symbol of vigour, prosperity and increase.

CAVE

You are finding your way into the more hidden reaches of your Deep Mind. If you have seen a tunnel leading onwards from the cave, 'ask' for another dream in which you can explore this. If no further way has been shown, 'ask' for more understanding of the present cave and then for a further way to be shown. The caves and caverns of your Deep Mind are limitless.

CEDAR

A prosperity symbol. A large, strong coniferous tree with wide-spreading branches and an invigorating fragrance. Its wood and oil have been noted from antiquity for their preservative qualities. General significances are stability, protection, health and longevity.

CEREALS

(Wheat, corn, rye, rice, millet or any other kind of edible grain). **A prosperity symbol.** All the good grains are so prolific in their growth and so healthful as a food that they are a natural symbol of abundance. Sesame rates special mention as a symbol – not only is it a highly nourishing cereal, it is also the famous 'key' to opening the treasure cave in the Arabian Nights tale of Ali Baba.

CELLAR

In dreams, often an alternative image for 'cave'. See **CAVE**.

CHART

You have reached a critical point in your progress and you need to consider what route to take. The dream symbol means you should indeed consider carefully. Here we see both 'destiny' and 'free will' in operation. You can only take one of the roads which are open to you – but it is entirely yours to choose which.

CHASM

See **ABYSS**.

CHESS

A game of chess in a dream indicates a struggle in winning your way to onward progress. You should ask yourself – *is your Creation of Prosperity becoming too entirely an effort of your conscious rational mind?*

CHEST

A receptacle for savings. It is for something which is already yours or coming to you, and which is to be kept secure.

CHILD

See **BOY**.

COINS

A symbol of gain: also a warning against 'thinking small'.

COLLAR

If you dream you are wearing a tight or uncomfortable collar and there is no obvious reason for this dream, it is an indication that you *are working too entirely with your head*, not as a whole person. Don't cut off the circulation from your emotions and your Deep Mind!

CORAL

You are developing your faculties in a way you may not yet be aware of. In dreams the sea represents the unconscious mind. Coral is a beautiful (and sometimes precious) substance which grows beneath the sea. So, whether in your dream you are shown it growing, or just a sample piece, be assured it represents some organized creative activity going on in your own depths.

CURTAIN

You are invited to go forward and open the curtain, but not to be impatient. Psychic events, or even earthly events, may need to mature before you can proceed as you wish.

DANCE

No matter how carefree it looks, every kind of dance has its style and its rules. So with the world of money. But – as in dancing – the more experience you have, the better you can enjoy the fun of it!

DAYBREAK

To dream of daybreak signifies a new hope, a new beginning at – probably many levels.

DEATH

No dream character ever really 'dies'. One's relationship with a particular person may end, or one may feel a particular aspect of oneself has been 'murdered' and any such happenings can be represented symbolically in a dream by a seemingly realistic corpse. *That rightly represents the dramatic way a part of your emotional nature feels about the matter.* If your conscious personality felt like that, you'd have had no need to dream it. Consider if there is anything you can or should do to alter the situation. If you don't think action is called for then just acknowledge the emotions that prompted the dream. Look them boldly in the face and move on.

DIAMOND

This supremely bright, hard and precious gemstone represents the high integrity of your inner being. It appears in dream either to confirm the rightness of your aspirations, or to certify that a desired project for which you are working psychically will indeed come to pass at the material level.

DIVING

The sea, as noted above, is an accepted dream-symbol of the unconscious mind. To dream of diving into it is to relax your mind, to refresh your psychic faculties, to take a brief vacation from the mechanisms of rationality. The more you enjoy the dream-experience of diving (and maybe of underwater exploring) the greater the indication of benefit to your psychic faculties.

DOLL

The appearance of this figure as a symbol in dream indicates that you are not taking seriously enough the development of your inner powers. Sometimes this shows a fear of being receptive and sensitive in psychic matters, sometimes simply a habit of preoccupation with external appearances which is not easily broken. But if you would be an advanced Creator of Prosperity – *bring the doll to life!*

DWARF

You may think of the dwarf figures of myth and legend who have mighty magical powers. You may think how in everyday life, people of small stature usually have the greatest energy and determination. There may be some project of yours which appeals to you, but you hesitate because it seems a small matter. If the dwarf symbol appears in your dreaming at this time, be assured that your project has tremendous potential if you give it energy and determination.

EAGLE

Powerful, high-flying, keen-sighted – the eagle appearing as a symbol in your dream shows you *either* that these words already figuratively describe you, *or* that you need to develop the qualities in question to pursue a project you have in mind. The further implication is that whether you recognize these qualities in yourself or not, you are fully capable of developing them.

EARTH

Positive: **A prosperity symbol.** To dream of earth in the natural state, fertile, flourishing, rich in metal ores and other minerals, is to dream of the material-level source of all increase. Even if you earn your income in the media, in interior design or in the higher echelons of commerce, somewhere along the line that income derives from people who gain it from the earth.
Negative: To dream of any of the distressful aspects of the condition of the natural world these days is a signal from your Deep Mind for waking action: both in ecological issues generally and because the stability of your own material affairs is involved.

ECLIPSE

To dream of the light of sun or moon being blocked from you is a warning. Don't cease to give heed to the power and life-sustaining properties of cosmic forces!

ELDORADO

The fabled Land of Gold is now and then the setting for pleasant dreams. You walk about picking up gold, silver and precious gems which seem perfectly real until you wake up. But this type of dream is a symbol of frustration, of lack of material opportunity for the Creator of Prosperity. It shows this is a time when you should look about, find a more productive use for your moneymaking talents.

EGG

If the egg is simply shown in dreams as a symbol, it is a reminder of the essential 'nest-egg'. If anything happens to the egg or there is any action concerning it in the dream, note and reflect upon what this tells you.

ENVELOPE

If a sealed envelope appears as a dream symbol, it signifies there is a surprise in store for you. The symbol can also imply that some information you want is in fact there in some area of your Deep Mind, but it will not be disclosed before the Deep Mind is ready.

FACE

Simply *a face* can appear as a symbol in dream. If it looks like a person known to you, you need to think what that person signifies in your life or your imagination. If it is an unknown face, you need to interpret its meaning from its expression – encouraging, anxious, and so forth.
If the face is quite expressionless, not animated, that is another matter: see **DOLL**.

FIRE

Intense energy and activity, supportive of life if directed, destructive if uncontrolled. Indicates a great time for action at all levels. Make sure your high energy level has enough creative outlets.

FLYING

See **AIRCRAFT**.

FOG

To dream of being in a fog means just what it looks like. You can't see where you are going. Also, if you try to move forward regardless, you may land into trouble. Best to have patience – it will probably not take long for the fog to clear, and then you will get a fresh view of things.

FORD

You are making your way to new prospects, keeping in touch with your Deep Mind and the ongoing 'feel' of things. This is a more sure procedure than making the crossing by 'bridge', in which you would have only the positive or negative feeling of the dream itself to guide you.

GARDEN

A garden symbolizes the borderland where the Deep Mind meets with the world of rationality. Its activities and images are not really artificial or contrived, but yet are guided rather than spontaneous. As in waking life, so in dream: one can relax without serious concern in a garden.

GEIGER COUNTER

May feature in the dreams of the Creator of Prosperity simply as a device for detecting a certain type of presence or occurrence. See **SONAR**.

GLACIER

Amid the heightened awareness and interaction of levels in a developing personality, a faint uneasy perception can arise, of lack of response in some area of the psyche. The sterile coldness of a glacier in the midst of a flourishing landscape gives a good image of this. However, the deep-level awareness of the unevenness of development which throws up the symbol, will of itself gradually activate the 'sleepy' faculties.

GLOVE(S)

The symbol of a glove, or of wearing gloves, in a dream indicates some lack of contact with an important reality. The symbol also indicates that the condition can easily be put right – since gloves are *removable*. If you don't at once locate the missing contact, a further dream may give a clue.

HIGHWAY

Mostly, driving along the highway is a simple expression of confident hope: the road to success! This dream indicates that all is going along well. Possibly, however, in your dream the highway seems a little too crowded for comfort? If that is the feeling of the dream, it suggests this is the time for you to do some new thinking, to look around (physically and psychically) for new lines of investment and enterprise.

HOLE

To see a hole as a dream symbol is a warning. Consider what sort of hole it is. Is it a hole in a street you might be walking or driving along? Or is it a hole in fabric – fabric which might symbolize the carefully woven texture of your plans? Either way, you need to identify that hole and either repair it or find another way around.

HONEY

A very apt and ancient **prosperity symbol**. The produce of the earth, the gleam of gold and the sweet taste of success.

ICE

See **GLACIER**

ISLAND

If finding yourself on a crowded highway suggests you should branch out a little on your own account, to find yourself on an island suggests maybe you should get back a little more with the crowd. This may not refer to the material level, however. The chief point is *not to get isolated psychically*.

LABYRINTH

See **MAZE**.

LADDER

As a dream symbol the ladder is a means of steep ascent to a new level of achievement. There is nothing essentially threatening about it, but its appearance indicates that effort is required in reaching a new goal. Consider your abilities and, if necessary, *strengthen them* before beginning the 'ascent'. But if you are confident of your powers and prepared for hard work, go ahead without hesitation.

LAMP

If a lamp is lighted for you, a light is cast on a subject which might have been 'obscure' to you. If you yourself light the lamp, you are shedding light for yourself and others.

LANDSLIP

This is an insecurity symbol which should be heeded. Even if you don't consciously see any cause to feel insecure in your surroundings (your job, your home, your financial ventures or even the possibility of an actual landslip) consider everything carefully to find where your Deep Mind perceives the threat. If you can find no cause for alarm, proceed as normal, but cautiously, and look for a further dream to explain matters. Not every threat of danger which arises in the astral world comes to material realization. But, for the time being, take care.

LEDGER

See **BOOK**.

LIGHTHOUSE

This signals a danger which has already been perceived and guarded against. It is also a sign of protection and safe-conduct. All you have to do is to move prudently and to stay where there is illumination and a clear way ahead.

MAZE

To see in dream either yourself or some anonymous person lost in a maze and unable to find the right path, signifies a real perplexity of mind. It indicates no danger however. There is simply a need to relax, to take a fresh view of the situation – and to call upon your deeper faculties to help you where your reason has been brought to a standstill.

METEORITE

To dream of the sudden appearance of a meteorite signals

the arrival, now or in the near future, of some factor in your affairs which is altogether alien to anything you had reckoned on. The feeling of the dream may give you a clue as to whether the surprise is pleasant or the reverse. If there is no such clue, patience is the best approach to the matter.

MIRAGE

The message of this dream symbol is simple: *don't be too quick to act upon a particular matter in accordance with the way it looks at first.* Wait and see how things shape before you respond.

NAKEDNESS

To be out and about in a dream, and suddenly to find that you are without any clothes, is a startling experience but need cause you no alarm. It does not for instance mean you are to be stripped of all you possess! Simply, this is one of those dream experiences which signal an early stage in the development of the faculty for astral projection – 'the out-of-body experience'. Not being used to the procedure, your astral self has gone forth as innocently as you came into the world, without a thought of clothing. Chances are, the shock of discovery snapped you back into wakeful consciousness. No harm done!

NAVIGATION

To dream you are steering any kind of boat or ship is a good sign. You are progressing forward, and you are in control. Your rational consciousness is, quite rightly, directing the voyage but the vessel is safely cradled in the waters – representing the fact that you are securely supported by your Deep Mind.

NEWSPAPER

To see a newspaper as a dream symbol is rather more literal than many such images. Whether in your dream you can read the headlines or not, it will be a good thing to take early notice of all the news during the next few days.

OCTOPUS

If you see this symbol in dream. It suggests something in the depths of your mind scares you. This can be because of the power of the factor in your Deep Mind to captivate your attention, maybe to turn you away from more current, profitable or extrovert interests. Only you can decide whether you *ought* to be scared of it or not. But don't let it turn you away from the whole vital world of your Deep Mind.

OIL WELL

This is certainly treasure from the depths! But don't mistake its symbolic nature. It represents a flow of powerful inspiration and creativity from far below the surface in your Deep Mind. Be ready to recognize it and to take full advantage of it.

ORCHARD

A prosperity symbol. An area of well-planned and well-ordered activity is progressing towards its timely fruition.

PHOTOGRAPH

In dreaming, to look at a photograph is very like looking into a mirror. No matter who or what type of person is shown there, it represents some facet or aspect of your own personality, whether known to you or not. If the photo is of a landscape or some natural object (tree, lake, mountain) it still characterizes some aspect of your personality. Whatever it is, your attention is being drawn to it for a purpose.

PIPELINE

To perceive a pipeline as a dream symbol shows you are conscious of a *channeling* of ideas and impulses from the Deep Mind.

POT OF GOLD

The legendary 'pot of gold' at the rainbow's end. Such an image in dream could warn you not to let all your creative imagery fulfill itself in the realms of dream and fantasy.

RACE

In some circumstances it can be vital to get in first. But in most resource-building, speed is not of the essence. If you are involved in a mater where quick action is vital, take note of every detail surrounding this dream symbol and consider what message it holds for you. If you are not thus involved, the dream can mean that you are becoming pressured needlessly.

RADAR

See **SONAR**.

RAILROAD

Like **RACE**, the railroad as symbol can imply that you are being pressured (or are pressuring yourself) into needless quick action. If no sense of stress is present, the dream conveys a meaning of steady progress on regular tracks.

ROOF

To have a dream in which it seems the roof over you is damaged or unsafe can be the result of a sense of insecurity from whatever cause. More specifically, it can show a feeling arising from your Deep Mind that something designed on purpose as a protection has become a source of danger. Take time therefore to look at your circumstances and see if this is the case.

SHORE

The edge of ocean or lake, or the edge of a river if the bank on which you stand is not much elevated above the level of the water: all are symbols of the psychic area where your Deep Mind and conscious mind meet. Anything which, in your dream, takes place in such a region is of special significance in your psychic work. If the dream shows you only that you are on the shore, psychically the significant happening is to be looked for soon afterwards – probably in your waking life.

SIEVE

Don't accept a business proposition which has just been put before you, or a plan you have just formulated, until you have examined it in every detail. Your conscious mind may be quite satisfied with it but your Deep Mind wants it sifted.

SISTER

You may dream that a sister of yours is helping in your Creation of Prosperity activities, when in earthly life this is not the case. The dream then indicates clearly that some existing or projected activity of yours will make a greater call on your psychic abilities than on your practical ones. If in fact you have a sister helping you, the meaning of the dream may still be as above, but you must judge by the circumstances.

SNAKE

To see in dream the symbol of an ordinary snake has always been regarded as warning of a hidden menace. A human-headed snake is however an ancient and powerful symbol of the unconscious. It signifies that the unconscious has a vital message for you. This message may be apparent from the content of the dream, or a further dream may be required to make it clear.

SONAR

Of all the detection devices which dream symbolism adopts from technology – the Geiger Counter, Radar, etc. – Sonar gives the most vivid likeness to the conscious mind's awareness of a new activity stirring far below in the vast caverns of the unconscious. If you are in process of establishing communication between the levels of your psyche, this symbol is a very promising indication.

SPEECH

To hear either yourself or another dream-character giving a speech is a sign that ideas are being sorted, are receiving clarification. Don't worry if you remember nothing coherent about the speech: the important thing is that the process is going on at a deep level where mere words usually mean little anyway.

STAIRWAY

In dreams the stairway is an *inviting* symbol. An upward leading stairway invites you to make progress at the present time: it will be an easy and well-regulated ascent. A stairway leading downwards invites you to closer understanding and communication with your Deep Mind. To see a stairway which goes both down and up from the point where you are is a sign that you already have a good awareness of the hidden levels beneath, and are ready to make a further and rapid upward progress *now*.

STAMPEDE

Whether of cattle, of wild horses, or of some other kind of animal, this symbol indicates that a lot of energy seems to have run to waste. It probably is nothing to worry about – maybe you've released a lot of pent-up anger you had built up for some reason, or a lot of frustration over an opportunity you were not free to take. Whatever it was, let it go and relax *now*. You are going to have good uses for your energy.

SUN

A prosperity symbol – *one of the greatest*. Sun or sunshine, this symbol represents that which ripens the harvests, the sustainer of all earthly life and increase. To have in your dream the unobstructed appearance of this symbol is a grand indication of your strong and direct link with the forces of abundance.

TECHNOLOGICAL DEVICES

Computer, Tablet, Smart Phone: any such technical devices appearing as symbols in your dreams denote special activity on the part of your Deep Mind to connect with your consciousness in the development of telepathy, clairvoyance or related psychic faculties.

TRUCK

A truck or similar vehicle on its way or arriving signifies good things coming to you. Although this may be an unexpected piece of luck, the method of its arrival will be solidly mundane and seemingly prosaic.

TOWER

Certainly for your Creation of Prosperity pursuits you need to take time off from a good many less useful (and often wasteful) occupations. But this symbol in your dream tells you to beware of cutting yourself off too much from family and friends.

VANDALISM

Damaged public property is always a sorry sight. To see this in your dream shows you have a deep apprehension of possible harm to your own personal assets. Make sure that everything is as secure as you can make it.

VAPOUR

See **FOG**.

WINGS

You are lifted into soaring flight by wings of inspiration, of hopeful purpose, of confidence in your developed abilities as a Creator of Prosperity. People who are developing powers of astral projection sometimes find themselves flying astrally and think it is a dream, but they generally fly *without wings*. Wings are a special symbol of your power to 'rise above' those earthly conditions which often hamper the advanced Creator of Prosperity. GOOD FLYING!

DENNING AND PHILLIPS

Melita Denning and Osborne Phillips are the joint authors of many successful and bestselling books on the development and practical application of the natural faculties of the psyche in dynamic relation to the living energies of the cosmos.

Their many years of study of Eastern and Western philosophies, of Jungian psychology and of the Classical Mystery Religions, and their practical experience of the spiritual techniques of the Western Mystery Tradition, amply qualify them as authorities in their field.

After spending eleven years in the United States, working with the President of Llewellyn Publications, Carl Llewellyn Weschcke, in the creation of a series of *practical guides* and other specific titles for Llewellyn, they relocated to United Kingdom in 1989.

Melita Denning passed away in 1997, shortly after the completion of her final joint work with Osborne Phillips: 'Entrance to the Magical Qabalah'.

In addition to his present revision and re-publication of 'Creative Moneymaking', Osborne Phillips has authored a number of further titles: on spiritual disciplines, on mediaeval history and on religious matters.

Printed in Great Britain
by Amazon